Getting Older
Never Looked So Good
A head to heels guide to ageless beauty

3JUDYS

SOUTHERN \ \ SPIKEY \ \ SASSY

D1455285

THRIVE Publishing®
A Division of PowerDynamics Publishing, Inc.
San Francisco, California
www.thrivebooks.com

ISBN: 978-0-9850828-8-8

Library of Congress Control Number: 2013937703

Printed in the United States of America on acid-free paper.

URL Disclaimer: All Internet addresses provided in this book were valid at press time. However, due to the dynamic nature of the Internet, some addresses may have changed or sites may have changed or ceased to exist since publication.

Table of Contents

This book is
dedicated...

to all the ladies who
refuse to give in to
gravity—or at least
don't let it show!

JUDY

"You may have to fight a battle more than once to win it."
Margaret Thatcher

You know that style is learned, but you may be driven wild by that *perfect dress* in the store window, and throw out all you know about your body. So give yourself room for errors, even expect them.

Just nudge yourself back to reality, and look again in your mirror and remember what looks *so good on your* body. You are a unique person made by God and you are beautiful inside and out.

Come on down, sit on my porch and have a glass of *Peach Tea.* Let us toast to you and all of us by kicking age to the curb and looking great!

Acknowledgements

The idea of *Getting Older Never Looked So Good* was the brainchild of Judith Taylor, aka Southern Judy. Knowing how many baby boomer women were hitting their fifty-year mark was the inspiration for writing a light-hearted approach to a serious subject on aging. Southern Judy remained focused and dedicated to launching this book, insisting the content remain relevant and encouraging. Her unyielding commitment and creativity motivated the other two Judy co-authors to step up to the plate and deliver the goods. Women in their fifties and beyond face completely different choices than during their younger years. One of these choices is how they look, feel and perform as they age. The three Judys are passionate about helping women be chic, stylish and savvy as they go through life's transitions.

Judith Herbert, aka Spikey Judy, was a treasure from the moment we connected with her. Coming from a background in new life and wellness coaching, Spikey Judy offers a unique blend of "whole-istic style" many women are eager to learn about and embrace. Spikey Judy's easygoing manner and California appeal makes her a great asset to this book and keeps the content easily relatable.

Judith Graham, aka Sassy Judy, was one of the early contributors. Her New York City style sense kept the other two Judys constantly aware that the book content needed to be authentic and fresh.

Coming from an entertainment background, Sassy Judy has a high style many women in their fifties feel they cannot justify. Sassy Judy not only gives them permission to explore this side of themselves, but also shows them how to do it.

Our publisher, Thrive Publishing, spearheaded by Caterina Rando, has a splendid team of experts and creative forces that gave this book its golden wings. Caterina's team provided a solid rock foundation that helped each Judy find her voice and set passion to paper. We three Judys are forever grateful to this team for helping us "thrive" in a book that once was only a dream.

To Susan Rich, our editor, whom we deeply appreciate for her enthusiasm and efficiency. Managing three women through book writing is probably similar to shooing flies at a picnic. On call duty—all day long.

To Tammy Tribble, our creative director, whose ideas and fun-loving approach gave this book its cleverness and class. We are so lucky to have you on our team. Right from the beginning, Tammy shared our vision of this book and provided the professional finesse we so much needed.

To our illustrator, DeMara Cabrera. She is an artist whose talent and speed whipping up illustrations gives this book its fun and flair. DeMara earned a master in fine arts, costume design from Boston University. Known for creating fabulous costumes for theatrical endeavors, we were thrilled when she agreed to do illustrations for our book. We admire DeMara for her patience and resilience as we three Judys requested revision upon revision. DeMara's gifts expand way beyond her design ability.

To the team who helped us look like BB's (beauty babes) Joanna Katz and David Gelezinsky of The Hair Parlour, NYC. Even though the salon was under construction, Joanna and David transformed their apartment to a beauty oasis on an early Sunday morning. What would we have done without their hair and makeup magic? To Henry O, our photographer, for taking our great cover shot. To Joel Borgella for creating our fabulous logo and designing our website. To Goldylocks, our Photoshop® queen, for erasing any slight, minor, little flaws we may have earned through the decades! We are imminently grateful to all of you.

This book could not have taken flight without the patience and understanding of our loving husbands. There were many late dinners, shortened conversations and attention to computers instead of the men in our lives. We appreciate your listening when needed and silence when requested. We are forever indebted to Mike, Greg and Austin who are the true wind beneath our wings. A simple thank you is not enough to express our deep appreciation of the support you gave us.

Finally, to our audience, baby boomer women who refuse to allow age to dim their light. We are deeply honored that you choose to age gracefully and gleefully. You are the inspiration for this book and we three Judys are committed to your well-being as well as your well-"heeling." May you glow with your own brand of sparkle because *getting older never looked so good!*

JUDY

One of my favorite quotes was said by Rosalind Russell in the movie Auntie Mame (1958). "Life's a banquet and most poor suckers are starving to death!" My favorite part of being a Baby Boomer is the varied and sumptuous buffet of life. Our generation of women were rebels who rejoiced in living their lives outside of the past gender definitions. We became mothers, doctors, lawyers, business tycoons, carpenters, mechanics and artists and some of us tried a little bit of all of these things. My advice to you, dear reader, is to feast upon all that life brings you. Your life is not winding down, it is taking off! Give yourself permission to showcase the unique you, embrace health and wellness in all aspects of your life, and, in the words of Auntie Mame, live, live, live!

Foreword

I bet it's as easy for you as it is for me to remember those days when walking out the door in tattered jeans, flip flops, hair loosely blowing in the wind and wearing not a stitch of makeup was oh-so-sexy. Remember that? I was in my early twenties, looked great in jeans and had a confidence that was buoyed by youth. They say it's natural to start losing our memory as we get older, but that's a feeling I'll never forget.

I haven't met a single woman who doesn't want that feeling now even as she faces 55, 65 or higher. We want to be attractive, yes, but feeling attractive is even more desirable. A client of mine once said, "Brenda, I'm 60, I'm not dead." No kidding!

My first book, *40 Over 40, 40 Things Every Woman Over 40 Needs to Know About Getting Dressed,* encouraged women to find their own style and wear what made them happy rather than seeking fashion advice from their cocky teenagers who were dying their hair purple and piercing body parts. Those 40-year-olds were equally afraid of looking like their own mothers.

Since then, 40 has been declared the new 30, 50 is the new 40 and I think 60 could easily be declared the new black. That's how much sense fashion and image make now! Relevant fashion advice is harder for the baby boomer to find and I understand the temptation to dress in age-inappropriate ways. We want to have our youthfulness. It's the juicy part of us that is as vital at 60 as it was at 20. Now how do we demonstrate our vitality, radiance and exuberance when our bodies have changed, clothes don't fit us the way they used to, and we're not even sure if products exist to serve our needs?

In my nearly thirty-year career in image consulting, I have known two of the three *Judys* for almost that whole time.

I admired Southern Judy well before we were even introduced. She was sitting near the front in a session room at an annual conference of the Association of Image Consultants International. I was across the aisle from her. She spoke up in the class, and I can still remember her grace, her style and her charm. When she spoke, her words were like butter. Not butter out of the refrigerator—no, room temperature butter, soft and creamy. Then I'd see her in the hallways. I couldn't help but notice the impeccable way she wore clothes in colors and fabrics that seemed to match exactly her gracious way of being in the world. She was a Southern woman and having grown up in North Dakota, I was captivated by this creature. You would be too.

Since I've gotten to know her better, every experience with her is like that first sighting. Whether it's a conversation at a conference about some of our favorite subjects, a phone call or an email, she is that same woman through and through. I would often get off the phone with her and imagine how lucky clients would be to have her on their side. No one could have a more devoted advocate than Southern Judy.

Then there's Sassy Judy. Oh my! I had the mind-expanding experience of serving on the International Board of AICI with this New York-based image consultant. Sassy Judy never walks into a room, she makes a grand entrance. How could she not? She's this tall, gorgeous woman with beauty pageant looks. I might have won Miss Congeniality back in 1970 at the North Dakota Junior Miss Pageant, however Sassy Judy is the real deal.

It's hard *not* to spot her at conferences. She's the tallest woman in the room. She knows how to wear high heels and a form-fitting red dress like no other woman. She owns her look. Her beauty has that siren quality. Would I love to have what she has? You bet! I'd love to be her roommate for a week and learn every trick and tip she uses that results in the confidence that she radiates.

The closest I've gotten so far is when we were gathered in Fort Worth, Texas for a strategic planning session with our board. No one could have missed the huge amount of bling on her finger—diamonds galore. I dug deep to find my bold voice and asked if I could try it on. Without hesitation, she slid it across the table to me. Unfortunately, I had to give it back, but for a bit, I got to enjoy a portion of the wattage that is Sassy Judy. I adore her!

Now the one Judy I haven't met yet is Spikey, and I feel like I already know her. We both live in California. We're near the same age, and although she rides Harleys® and I've only sat on one, I love her "whole-istic" view of women and style.

Can you imagine how excited I am that these three incredible *Judys* are opening up their beauty/body/style tool kit and showing us what's inside? I'm deliriously excited about what they have to share with all of us baby boomers. Their geographical mix touches all the bases for women our age. They are as devoted as I am about showing women how to be their best and how to live their best starting from right here, right this moment. For those of us who can't wait to devour their tips and insights, this triple scoop of *Judys* is the yummiest treat yet. Getting older never looked so good, you say? Bring it on!

Brenda Kinsel, AICI CIP
Author, *40 Over 40, 40 Things Every Woman Needs to Know About Getting Dressed,* www.brendakinsel.com

JUDY

As I look back at five decades I realize my accomplishments were inspired by the people who made a difference in my life. Some have entered my life for a reason, some for a season and some for a lifetime. I have learned both divine and difficult lessons from these precious souls. Now is the time for me to make a difference in other people's lives. I am honored and humbled to share the gift of beauty, empowerment and enlightenment with each of you.

Hair Now!
Hair Now!

"Beauty Parlor: A place where women curl up and dye."
—Peter Sanger, author of *Aiken Drum*

What is it about baby boomer hairstyles we can spot from the top of the Empire State Building? Something is missing—fullness, texture, shine. Is it asking too much to have luscious locks at our age? We don't think so, and we are prepared to tell you how boomer manes can be beautiful. We begin by asking a few questions. Ready, set, spray!

When was the last time you changed your hairstyle? Is your hairstyle *convenient* or *current*? Would you consider an edgy new cut or tossing in hair extensions? Which is more flattering on you—short or longer hair? Should you dye or dye not? What can rescue thinning hair? Should you color your gray? Some stylists say we should alter our hairstyle every six months—even if it's as simple as changing a part. Could it be you are a bit "set" in your hair care?

It's not a secret that as we age, our hair changes in texture and fullness. The 3 C's—color, cut and conditioning—are exactly what we need to have a great hairstyle. Is your hairstyle up-to-date or a bit dated?

In this chapter, Southern Judy explains what every self-respecting woman down South knows about keeping up hair care and it starts with hair color. She not only tells you what to color but how to color. She even gives advice on how to get your hair color looking young and desirable. I never thought of hair looking desirable though I learned *this* is a Southern tradition.

Spikey Judy takes a look at everything from casual California hairstyles to Hollywood glam styles. She talks about modernizing an old style. She has great advice about perms, straightening hair, hair products and styling tips. She'll have you thinking about styles you would probably never consider. Even I may try a spike or two in my hair instead of on my heels.

Sassy Judy, that's me, has the New York City slant on haircuts. I explain exactly what *meno-hair* is and how to avoid it. I tell you why boring, banker safe, blunt cuts are just not flattering. I let you know when long is too long and when short is too short. Finding a good stylist to cut your hair takes effort. In New York, if you don't have a chic cut you had better steer clear of Fashion Avenue.

How exactly how do we find what works with the hair that now possesses us?

It begins with an honest discussion with your inner goddess. Are you in a time warp? Do you refuse to cut your ponytail? Does your hair color look like it came from a paint can? Do you have one of those fried, dyed and shoved-to-the-side hairdos? Do you believe that as we age we should go lighter in hair color?

We know we can't hide our age but we can update our look. Since our hair is generally the first thing people notice about us, it's time we trump up those tresses. Our hair labels us as healthy and contemporary and it can also shout *mature* and *matronly*. Does your hair identify who you really are? All of us can use a "brush-up." Here is our style file of suggestions for diva-licious locks.

JUDY

Is This Hair to Dye for?

By Southern Judy

"I'm not offended by all the dumb-blonde jokes because I know that I am not dumb. I also know I'm not a blonde."
—Dolly Parton, singer, entrepreneur

The truth is we could all use a bit of color. They say that only your hairdresser knows for sure, that's not totally true. The fact is that our hairdresser cannot keep a secret.

Honey, down South it is mandatory to, may I say, keep up appearances. Now, did we say that we could not improve on what the good Lord gave us? Hush now, I am talking about *adding* a strand or two of another color. Most women know this as a *weave*. For us baby boomers it is *frosting* or *highlights*.

As my mother would say, "The apples should not fall far from the tree," meaning that you should stay as close as you can to the color you were born with. Does this mean you cannot or should not change your hair from its natural color? Heavens no, however hues that complement your skin and eye coloring work best and are more flattering for you.

Fair skin tends to look best with lighter shades: blonde, light brown, strawberry blonde, and some shades of red. Darker skin tones need darker shades of brown or deep mahogany reds. Careful here that you do not go too dark or you will look like Elvis, or my neighbor Mrs. Evans. God knows that woman dyes her hair as dark as midnight on a cold winter's night! Think about Cher for a moment and how her newest look as a blonde does not complement her skin and eyes as well as her trademark look of long dark hair.

Blondes have more fun they say, and it may be true. I was born a natural blonde, and all my childhood I had dreams of darker hair. Now those days remind me that I would have had blonde roots.

As baby boomers, when we see signs of gray hair it makes us want to run to the local store, pick a color and try to fix our hair at home. Note to the wise: this is a serious step to tackle all by yourself. Magazines are great resources and will give you some ideas of color and style. You should schedule a consultation with your hairdresser. She has a wealth of knowledge on the colors that would be the best choice for you and your lifestyle.

There is a lot of talk lately about showing your roots—this is when your hair is growing out and that band of gray or black needs to be colored. This seems like the trendy thing to do, but to me it's like showing the hem of your slip. This is a fine line you are walking. Remember, showing a little bit of roots goes a long way to spoiling your perfect style.

So can you change your hair color? Absolutely and have fun doing it. Nothing says "younger looking" than a crisp color that brightens your face and your attitude.

\\\|//
JUDY

Hair Style: Barely There or Hair to Spare?

By Spikey Judy

"If I want to knock a story off the front page,
I just change my hairstyle."
—Hillary Rodham Clinton, Former First Lady

California girls are portrayed as laid back, sun worshipping, granola eating, yoga practitioners. Do these surfer and biker babes need to worry about their hair? Yes! Californians might have a reputation for being casual, however our movie star culture still expects us to have perfect hair even under not-so-perfect conditions. Whether sweating on the beach or in the gym, every day needs to be a good hair day. If you live in California, you should be able to ride your Harley® for 100 miles, pull over, take off your helmet and shake out your perfect, glorious locks of thick blond hair. Alas, most women look more like Cruella De Vil after a long bike ride.

Aside from having a slew of stylists following behind on their Harleys®, how does today's active baby boomer maintain hair that looks casual, yet not out of control? Our mothers' solution was to spend the day in rollers and then use industrial-grade hairspray to hold their hair in place. A tease here and a flip there, followed by a good thirty seconds of spraying and they were good to go. Rebellious boomers threw out the hairspray and either chopped their locks into mod pixies or wove flowers into long hair.

Fortunately, there are alternatives to cement head or going *au natural*. Choose a good hairstyle that works with your face shape and lifestyle. Always select hair products that work with your natural hair. For thinning hair—the curse of aging—opt for a lighter hair gel or mousse that adds natural fullness. Purchase products with *clean* or *light hold* in the description. Be careful not to overuse any product or you might end up with gooey clumps of hair. Usually just a pea-sized amount is sufficient. Also, do not over-wash your hair. Shampooing strips your hair of its natural oils, which is something else we lose as we age. Use a lightweight hairspray for a more natural look.

For those really bad hair days, think about purchasing some fun hats. I love hats and they can do wonders for covering up lackluster, unhappy tresses. I have very fine, thin, naturally curly hair that turns into a big frizzy puff in the humidity. I love a good beret as it can be worn several ways and is also great in rainy weather. Just be prepared to hear everyone say *bonjour* to you.

If you really want some hat inspiration, check out the Idiosyncratic Fashionistas at www.idiosyncraticfashionistas.blogspot.com. These ladies really know how to wear hats.

Lastly, I wouldn't be living up to my name if I did not give you some tips for a good spikey look. Traditionally, the punks used egg whites to achieve their awesome spiked Mohawks. Thankfully, today there are products that don't require us to separate eggs. Make sure you have some short pieces of hair to work with. After washing, work a tiny amount of texture cream into your hair. Blow dry using your fingers to work the spikes. You can also use a straightening iron to further accentuate the spikes. Twirl a sticky gel through your locks, then follow up with a firm hold hairspray—I like Paul Mitchell® Freeze and Shine Super Spray®. Hold the spikes out and spray at the roots.

Make every day a good hair day. Invest in good hair products, pick up a couple of fun hats and choose a hairstyle that complements both the inner and outer you. Let your crowning glory be glorious.

JUDY

Your Hair Cut: Hippie Hair or Menopause Hair?

By Sassy Judy

"People get real comfortable with their features. Nobody gets comfortable with their hair. Hair trauma. It's the universal thing."
—Jamie Lee Curtis, actress, spokeswoman

What do haircuts and hot flashes have in common? I wish I'd never have one again! Most women in New York would rather have heartburn than a hair cut. The minute we see the scissors we bow our heads and pray, "please, cut it right!" Because in New York one has to have a great cut to remain even on the D-list society register. The problem is it's harder than catching a cab during rush hour to get the right cut as we age.

You would think, living in New York every baby boomer woman would have a fabulous haircut. Some swear by their high-end Madison Avenue salons—although they never look any better when they're finished. It's just the same old blown-out bob cut. Why? Because getting these women to try a new haircut is like getting them to pay retail for clothes. Yet New Yorkers of every age are judged by their haircuts.

Meno Hair – can we say "old" any other way?

Is your hair somewhat fine and thin in texture? Then you may be a candidate for a short, chic cut. However, take a good look at your profile. Are your neck and chin relatively firm and taut? If so, short will look great. If not, have your hair cut to a length that frames your face and draws attention away from these problem areas.

Here's the trap some women fall into: Meno-hair! What is it? Meno-hair is when the hair is cut super-short with no style whatsoever—like a buzz cut—to seemingly ward off hot flashes. We know it doesn't work but there's an element we boomers need to fight against, that of giving up and giving into old age. Really, we can do much better than that! Think of socialite Kris Jenner and her sexy, short do. She looks terrific, feminine and hot! Yes, we know Kris is well preserved, but heck—we can be that way, too.

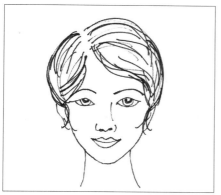

Short and chic – younger looking

The bob, bob, bob keeps bobbin' along!

Lose the hippie hair. True, coarse, thick hair looks great longer. But you don't want to grow it so long that you look young from behind and old in the front. Who do you think you're kidding? This is a common mistake made by hippie hair women who looked fine during the sixties, yet not fine as they are nearing *sixty*.

Hippie hair gone wrong

Layers are flattering and fresh

Is your hair fairly healthy, yet thinner than it used to be? Learn how to snap in a few hair extensions. These will make a good hair day better. The trick here is to know when too much is too much. You can look like one of the *Real Housewives of Hookerville* in a New York minute! So don't over "do" it.

A tip before you get any new haircut is to collect celebrity photos of women whose hair texture is similar to yours. That way both you and your stylist will have a reference point. It also helps your stylist to determine if what you want will work with your hair texture.

Having a great haircut is like having a great fitting bra. Nothing lifts your mood more. Don't get stuck in a rut with the same old cut. Start with a head-to-heart talk with your stylist and give him or her a chance to do something fresh and new. And remember, it takes thirty days to break an old habit. Put a lock on your inner chatter—the one that is afraid of change—and instead enjoy a latte with your friends.

Now go get that dashing cut that brings out the star you are!

Southern Says...

JUDY

- Leave-in conditioner is the best product for your dry hair.
- Combed in lemon juice and water will lighten your hair in the sun.
- Use a comb with large openings when combing wet hair.
- Get a wig the same style as your hair and wear it on a bad hair day.

Spikey Says...

JUDY

- Hair color, especially reds, will fade quicker in the sunlight. Use a leave-in hair protector that contains a sunscreen. I use Paul Mitchell® Color Protect® Locking Spray.
- Add highlights and lowlights to add dimension. This also gives the illusion of thicker hair.
- If you are not sure how a new color or style will look on you, try on some wigs. Now you can road test looks without succumbing to scissors or dye.
- Want to add a fun shock of color to your hair? Try some of the new clip-on hair extensions—these come in bright purples, blues, greens, and pinks.

Sassy Says...

JUDY

- In between color? Keep your roots fresh using a black/brown mascara wand or blonde eyebrow wand.
- Beer hair anyone? Try using warm beer to add volume (the hops and malt do this) and shine as beer coats the hair strands! When it comes to hair, beer holds its liquor!
- Hold the heat! When blow-drying hair use medium heat instead of hot. It may take a few extra minutes but the result is thick locks versus limp locks.
- Style your hair in the opposite direction you have been doing. You won't believe the difference in volume.

This Mirror Cracks Me Up!

"I am a reflection of you. Well, not an exact reflection,
I don't have wrinkles."
—*Mirror Mirror,* the movie

We baby boomer women turned our backs on our mothers' notions of beauty in favor of baby oil and skimpy bikinis. When we looked in the mirror, we saw youth, rebellion and freedom. What do we see now? Wrinkles, age spots and droopy eyelids. In other words, our mothers' faces staring right back at us!

The market is full of products that promise us eternal youth in a bottle. Advertisers use Photoshop® to age a young model. The model then allegedly uses some kind of miracle cream and, voila, is shown sans wrinkles and other bothersome signs of aging. If it were that easy, we could download our faces onto the computer and digitally edit away old age. Do we then buy in to the promises of the beauty industry and spend thousands of dollars chasing youth, or do we just give up and avoid looking in the mirror?

In this section we face the mirror head-on, addressing the problems of aging faces while offering up a few fabulous recommendations.

Southern Judy takes a no-nonsense look at wrinkles and encourages us to step up to the mirror and acknowledge that we are indeed aging. Burying your head in the sand is not going to make the lines go away—although sandblasting your face via microdermabrasion does help! Southern gets us off our front porches by offering some easy and common sense tips to lose the wrinkles. She even gives us a suggestion for dealing with the funky-looking saggy skin between "the girls."

Spikey Judy, that's me, explores the world of skincare and offers up a decidedly California—granola eating/Yoga poser—solution to repairing skin damage and reversing the signs of aging. I challenge you to recognize that the skin is attached to the rest of our body and needs the same care we would give our hearts or other important organs. The key to the Fountain of Youth is first found through a healthy diet and exercise. I also promote a habit of good skincare through daily cleansing and moisturizing and periodic visits to a professional esthetician.

Sassy Judy, our New York diva and makeup artist extraordinaire, gives us her expert insights on makeup. She urges women to paint their faces, but do so in a way that plays down signs of aging and allows our inner beauty to shine forth. She tackles some of the more challenging aspects of makeup and aging, including selecting a foundation and eye shadows, working with shrinking and quirky eyebrows, concealing problem eye areas, and—my personal favorite—getting rid of those nasty lines around the lips.

So buckle up and join us in our journey through the looking glass and into the not-so-wonderful land of aging skin. You will emerge through the other side looking and feeling a lot younger.

JUDY

Wrinkles—About Face —Not on My Face!

By Southern Judy

"Jewelry takes people's minds off your wrinkles."
—Sonja Henie, Norwegian figure skater and film star

Most of the time we can ignore a pound or two, at least with lots of coffee. It is the lines I am seeing on my face that make me want to drink the whole pot and just sit on the porch that have me concerned.

Mind the wrinkles? Heavens yes! It is one more sign of getting older. Just last year I hid the birthday candles and pretended they did not exist over the count of forty, or at least not in my box.

Giving up and not trying, is something I refuse to allow you or me to do. They used to call it snake oil and it seemed to cure every problem you thought you had. Now the newest and latest glass jar costs more and claims to outdo all the products Aunt Irene has used for more than a decade.

Is there any truth to the claims of products that deliver a more youthful, less lined face?

Honey listen, does the slogan, "We have come a long way, baby" mean anything to you? I guess I would have to just sit on the porch longer if I did not believe in modern chemistry. Not in the formula, but in the chemists. They are getting wrinkles too, so I *know* they are working long hours discovering the Fountain of Youth, putting it in a bottle, and then on display at your local cosmetic counter.

We all know that our skin changes over the course of time. It is proven that drier skin wrinkles and shows age faster, so adding moisturizer to your daily regimen is a no-brainer. Our battle against wrinkles has been going on since Cleopatra's time and the fighting has not slowed down yet.

Wrinkles show up in the craziest places. For instance, take your décolleté—yes, right on your chest and between your boobs. There is something just not fair about this area, how visibly it shows your age. Try this tip: after your nightly rituals, wash your décolleté with water and leave a little damp. Rub some of your favorite mineral oil, I prefer extra virgin olive oil myself, into your décolleté. In the morning you will be surprised to see some of those pesky wrinkles are gone.

Hormonal changes also create wrinkles, so you might want to talk about hormone replacement therapy next time you visit your doctor.

Here are some ideas to try if you have noticed your skin is a little drier.
- Apply rich night creams after cleansing your face before bed.
- Cotton pillowcases are stiff and can press wrinkles into your skin over time. Cotton can also rub off your outer eyebrows. Instead, choose synthetic—better yet, satin—pillowcases.

- Going to bed with makeup on ages your face. If you do go to bed without first taking off your makeup then your partner had better be worth it!

Expecting the wrinkles to go away by themselves is like expecting rain to fall in the desert. Why not bring the rain to you? Try these tips, pamper your skin with extra moisturizers and watch some of the lines fade away.

As famed entertainer Mae West used to say, *"An ounce of performance is worth pounds of promises."*

JUDY

Skincare: Does Snake Oil Really Work?

By Spikey Judy

"She got a mudpack and looked great for two days. Then the mud fell off."
—Henny Youngman, British-American comedian

The Beach Boys immortalized California girls in a song: "The West Coast has the sunshine and the girls all get so tanned." In our youth, we spent hours in the sun, slathered with baby oil. The consequence is that we now live with leathery, wrinkly, old lady skin. More troublesome is that the damage is not limited to the surface of our skin, but also affects us on a deeper cellular level. This can lead to the

Big C—cancer. It is no wonder that the home of the beach bunny also contains one of the largest concentrations of skincare specialists and plastic surgeons who promise us miracle treatments that will give us back our youthful looking skin.

Are these snake oil salesmen correct? Yes—sort of. It is possible to reverse the damage to our skin and achieve a healthier and more youthful complexion. The good news is that you do not have to spend a fortune.

If you were diagnosed with high cholesterol, you would focus on improving your heart health. The same goes for our skin. It is our largest bodily organ, yet we often overlook the benefits of a healthy lifestyle for skincare. Think carefully about what you put in your body. Eat lots of fresh raw fruits and vegetables, especially those rich in vitamins A, C and E. Omega 3s, like those found in salmon, are excellent for your skin. Dark chocolate can reduce skin roughness and has other health benefits as well, so let's pause for a chunky bite.

Guess what? Our bodies are made up of about 57 percent water, so drink up. Keeping your body hydrated will add moisture to your skin. Don't forget to exercise! I bet you were hoping I would forget to mention the E-word. Exercise keeps your body and your skin toned, plus helps rid you of toxins that can contribute to a dull and unhealthy looking complexion.

While diet and exercise are critical to healthy, more youthful-looking skin, don't throw out your skincare products with the bathwater. Make sure to cleanse your face in the morning when you get up and in the evening before you go to bed. Use a product that will clean your skin without stripping its natural oils. For daytime, use a moisturizer with sunscreen. While the majority of sun damage occurs in childhood, don't exacerbate the problem by further irradiating your face. Use a richer moisturizer in the evening, but not something that leaves greasy marks on your pillow.

Say yes to facials. Exfoliating, especially with chemicals, is the best way to remove dead skin cells. Avoid giving yourself a deep facial as you can cause permanent damage to your skin. Instead, make an appointment with a licensed esthetician. Monthly facials are a wonderful treat, and try to have a deep facial—microdermabrasion or chemical peel—at least once every three months. An experienced skincare professional also has treatments for those nasty brown spots that are your skin's way of protecting you from UV radiation. Professional care will help your skin look and feel smoother and younger.

Remember, beauty may be more than skin deep, but our skin is what people see first. Take care of it!

JUDY

Makeup: Less Is More, More Is Less, or More or Less?

By Sassy Judy

"Nature gives you the face you have at twenty; it is up to you to merit the face you have at fifty."
—Coco Chanel, French designer

Every morning, millions of New Yorkers hit the coffee counter. For me, I hit the makeup counter. I transform from frump to fab and I'll do this as long as I can put my fingers in a pot and paint my face. And when it's my turn to die, my makeup artist will be the first one in the morgue. Wearing makeup is like losing ten pounds—it makes you look terrific!

Most women don't share my passion for makeup, but that's not an excuse not to wear any. It gets cakey when I see women pack on too much and it's just scary when no makeup is worn at all. Calvin Klein once said, "The best thing is to look natural, but it takes makeup to look natural."

As we age, our natural coloring becomes paler: Our skin, hair and eyes fade, and that's why we need a makeup update. As for me, I can always tell the age of a woman by the color of her lipstick. The young ones wear a tinted lipgloss, if that, and older women wear bright pinks and corals that are creamy or matte. It's not just the color that tells your age, it's the consistency, too.

Here are a few makeup tips that help you look your best as you get older.

- **Foundations today** are multi-taskers containing sunscreens, hydrators, smoothers, lifters and reflectors all in one package. Don't think of your skin type—oily, dry, combo—think instead of your skin tonality—light, medium, deep—and you'll discover the perfect blend that looks *skinsational.*
- **When it comes to eye shadows** most of us shudder at shimmers because they accentuate our fine, and not so fine, lines. Try a gel liner pencil to emphasize your eyes. Go easy on the shadows, choose only silky matte powders.
- **Eyebrows make me bristle too.** As we age our brows either thin

out or they get bushy and wiry. Grooming them can be harder than sitting in a pencil skirt, and we don't want to end up looking like Joan Crawford. Find a combination of pencils and powders that fill in *only* the areas that are thin or bald. Brush the brows upward for an eye-lifting look.

- **Where's the "lip luck" in a jar?** All of us experience thinner lips and those dreadful vertical lines that bracket our pout. No cosmetic company has solved this issue to my satisfaction, however there is an age-old makeup artist secret to soften these lines. First, apply foundation on your lips and dust with a thin sheet of powder. Next apply your lipstick and then line with a lip liner. Finally, place a tissue over your lips and "blast" the tissue with a powder brush loaded with loose powder. Yes, the powder will permeate the tissue. The powder applications diminish fine lines and make your lip color last longer.

- **Eye concealer is another eye sore.** Use a sheer foundation with radiance qualities instead of concealing ones. These foundations contain ingredients that reflect light away from the hollows of the eyes. Apply under the eye area *and* follow the contour of the cheek to the side of the nose. Voila—what a glow!

Extreme is just that – extreme

Just enough is always younger looking

Ok ladies, makeup works miracles as long as you wave your magic wand. Why not dump those drawers of old paints and powders and start with just one new product? When you've mastered that, keep adding a new one until you've updated your look. Don't forget, a little makeup, a little paint, makes you look like what you ain't!

Southern Says...

 JUDY

- Concealer in the corner of your inner eye takes darkness away.
- Use eye shadow, the same color as your hair for your eyebrows. This makes a softer more natural look.
- Vaseline® makes a great lip gloss in a pinch.
- Emollient day creams rated SPF 30 or better. Never miss a day, even during winter months. Sunshine on naked skin is simply not done in the South.

Spikey Says...

 JUDY

- How about some instant Botox® without needles? Try Hydroxatone® 90 Second Wrinkle Reducer. This serum really works to reduce the appearance of wrinkles. It even fills in shallower creases. Do not move your face while the serum is drying.
- Diminish the appearance of deeper wrinkles with a highlighter pencil. Use the highlighter directly on the wrinkle or crease.
- If you forgot your eyebrow pencil and need a touchup, a Number 2 pencil works great and the color works for most complexions.
- Use your eye cream on those nasty lines above the lips.

Sassy Says...

 JUDY

- Instant facelift? Wear cat-eye glasses and sunglasses. Meow!
- Super dry, chapped face? Use A&D ointment—the same stuff used on a baby's butt for diaper rash! It works, I would know!
- Want that JLo glow? Use a light-reflecting concealer like YSL® Touché Eclat. Apply under the eye, blending along the nose into smile lines. Secrets of celebs!
- Never use mascara on lower lashes unless you are channeling raccoons!

The Upper Third:
Necks, Arms and Breasts

"After thirty, a body has a mind of its own."
—Bette Midler, American actress, singer

Ignorance is forgiven to a point, after that stupid takes over. Sure, you say, she is blonde—and I am—just don't think that means my head is in the sand. Simply put, in the South we cover things up!

Of course only our bathroom mirror would have proof that we are anything less than our svelte selves. Should I die on the street, my attorney will swear in court that my body was on the beach in Italy—perfectly toned and tanned. That body found on the street simply was not mine!

In this chapter, Spikey Judy reminds us that if our aging arms jiggle like Jello® when we cruise on our Harley®—it is possible to slim our wings without trimming our style.

Turkey neck is truly a fate worse than death. It makes our wardrobe shift from low neck looks to something Hollywood women have known for years as a gift from God: the scarf. We can claim it is windy or that it matches the dress—but the truth is scarves work in a pinch to cover what we do not want seen.

Sassy Judy gives some good tips on keeping our necks on a leash and trying to hang in there, no pun intended. The fact is, we all will have to endure and find our own way of keeping our chin up. The British have the "stiff upper lip" thing cornered, maybe they know something we don't.

Protecting our upper half from sagging requires a serious defense strategy and we will do whatever it takes to support our neck, arms and breasts until a better way, a newer cream or a special exercise is discovered. All this before we use the last resort—the dreaded knife!

I am in my studio, deep in the South, looking at a saying:

> ***"Youth is a gift, AGE is an ART"***
> —author unknown

Oh, how we try. . .sure we have the creams, lotions and potions. We also have something that the youth do not have, *money,* and we are willing to spend it.

Honestly, we see our flaws and are more critical of ourselves than others. Okay, not everyone: Our local know-it-all, Sarah Mae Lewis, has something to say about *everything,* including the arms and neck of our beloved Aunt Nellie, who has been around since the Roaring Twenties. As the story goes, Aunt Nellie found the most beautiful sleeveless floral dress with a low neckline. I know, I hear you saying, "What was she thinking?" There was Aunt Nellie out and about and Sarah Mae sees her parading around downtown. Words that cannot come out of *my* mouth were heard by most of the church choir.

Lesson learned: Low necks and sleeveless dresses are best worn by women who stay at the gym night and day...after they pass the forty-year mark.

All you have to do is look in the magazines and see the ads on television to know there are new ways right off the press that promise the latest and best ways to assist us in our battle against the jiggles, turkey neck and wavy arms. You can bet that we—Spikey Judy, Sassy Judy and me, Southern Judy, will be out in the trenches fighting for you all the way.

JUDY

Got a Turkey Neck?
Quit Necking Around!

By Sassy Judy

"Now that's a neck!"
— French-born American Vogue magazine editor Diana Vreeland
after seeing the model, Iman

Ugh, I hate my fifty-something neck. In our forties we get wrinkles and in our fifties we get turkey necks. Oh, what can be done about that wobble gobble flesh that hangs down and destroys our beautiful jaw line? In New York we see aging babes pulled up tighter than their Spanx® control panties. Some of them have had so much work done they look downright alien. We don't want to look freaky, so what can be done about our sagging chins and turkey necks?

I wear my hair short, so having a sculpted neckline is serious business to me. Surgery? Not for me, at least not now. I'll hop on the subway at midnight before I go under the knife. Years ago I tried wearing a chinstrap to alleviate my double chin. The only thing that got lifted was my bank account. Next I tried neck creams. Some of them burned, some dried and cracked before washing them off and some melted—yuck! I tried the old routine of slathering on some miracle cream and massaging my neck in upward motions only to see the same old sag. Really, with all the advanced treatments available there must be something that deals with turkey necks besides a hatchet!

For years I've literally been sticking my neck out to find non-invasive solutions for a nice neckline. Here's what I know.

Neck Exercises
There are a few yoga-cises that tone and firm the neck area. Try the Jim Carrey neck jut. Just stick out your neck as far as you can and tense the muscles like cords several times. Another exercise is to tilt your head up, put your tongue to the roof or your mouth, smile, then swallow. This one's a bit of a contortion, but you definitely feel the stretch. These exercises are not going to give you back your youth. As with any workout, you will see improvements if you do them regularly.

Neck Creams
Some say this is a waste of time and money, yet cosmetic companies keep inventing new and improved creams that are effective. Look for a neck cream that helps improve collagen and elastin production on the dermis layer. Before you buy, do your online research. Key in "neck treatment creams" and a whole slew of products and

comparisons will pop up. This information constantly changes as technology advances. Also, never use your eye cream on your neck. Your neck deserves its own special formula to battle wrinkling, crinkling and drooping.

Non-invasive Treatments

These will not give you the results of a surgical facelift, although they do offer some improvement. Success here depends in part on the amount of loose skin you have. Don't bother with treatments intended for thirty-somethings, you will be disappointed. The very latest technology is called Ultherapy®. It uses ultra sound waves to penetrate the dermis and epidermis. I tried it myself and was satisfied with the outcome. After treatment, firming continues over the next several months, with overall results lasting up to two years. The cost is about half the amount of a facelift. Except for the oxycodone that made me quiver, the procedure itself was as easy as ordering a pizza—I went to a birthday party that same night.

Surgery

Facelifts can run upwards of $7,000. I've known ladies who go to Mexico to save money on this procedure. Are you kidding? No nickel and diming on my neck! Be certain to go to a board certified surgeon whose work you have seen. Don't forget to factor in the post-surgery downtime, too.

When it comes to neck flab, do your homework and know your options. Before you sign up for a facelift, consider less invasive options, and be sure to check out Spikey's and Southern's advice, too. Who knows, maybe you'll invent a new chinstrap that holds that neck up high!

JUDY

Arm Candy? It's Not Sweet if It Jiggles Like Jelly

By Spikey Judy

"Come and giggle while you jiggle in a wiggling spree."
—Jell-O® Brand Gelatin commercial

I looked so cool on my brand new cruiser—leather chaps, sexy tank top and to-die-for biker boots. I owned it as I pulled up to the intersection, exhaust pipes rumbling. As I waited for the light to change, I caught a strange movement out of the corner of my eye. The loose skin on my arms had taken on a life of its own and was performing a quasi-belly dance in rhythm with the vibrating motorcycle.

Wiggly gelatin is cute, jiggling upper arms are not. Gravity, loss of skin tone and weight fluctuations give baby boomer women wings. Unfortunately, we're not flying high with these icky, flabby things, but what can we do about it? Do we limit ourselves to sweating it out in long sleeves year-round? Covering the loose bits is one solution, but don't rush to clean out your closet just yet. Alternatives to clothing choices include toning, surgery and ink.

It is never too late to tone your arms. Focus on the triceps, the large muscle on the back of the upper arm. There are many exercises that target the triceps including pushups. My favorite triceps workout is boxing. A well-thrown punch creates a twisting motion that results in lean and toned arms. There is also nothing better for working out frustrations, especially the hormonal ones, than hitting a punching bag.

No matter what exercise you choose, invest in a couple of sessions with a personal trainer. A trainer will make sure that you are performing an exercise correctly, maximizing—or in this case minimizing—results. Additionally make sure to feed your muscles with lean protein and lots of water.

Exercise is great for toning arms, although not the ultimate solution if you have lost a tremendous amount of weight and are left with excess skin—think of Oprah Winfrey and her infamous bat wings. In some cases, surgery provides the best solution. The most common procedure is an arm lift or brachioplasty. A surgeon makes an incision extending from the elbow to the underarm, and sometimes on to the side of the chest. Liposuction might also be used to remove excess fat. The patient is left with a firmer more youthful looking arm. The downside is a long, conspicuous scar. If you are considering surgery, consult with a member of the American Society of Plastic Surgeons.

In addition to toning and surgery, what about adding a little ink? Tattoos are becoming more mainstream and offer a unique option for blah arms. A top Southern California tattoo artist has the following recommendations when considering ink.

- Tattoos are permanent so choose with care. Select a design that has deep personal meaning.
- Aging skin has a tendency to cause the ink to travel, resulting in unwanted lines. Avoid intricate designs; instead opt for more organic patterns.
- A good design flows with anatomy, not against it. For arms, select a tattoo that follows the shape of the arm, not one that cuts straight

across. Like clothing, the tattoo should accentuate the best parts of the body.

- Disclose all medications you are taking to the tattoo artist. Some medicines contain blood thinners and can cause excessive bleeding during the procedure.
- Be aware that aging skin requires additional healing time and there may be some bruising.

Whether you tone up, clip your wings or add ink, proudly roll up your sleeves and do something about those upper arms. There's a sexy halter dress calling your name.

JUDY

Bare Breasted?
Bra Fitter, Give Me a Lift!

By Southern Judy

"This girl single-handedly could make bosoms a thing of the past."
—Billy Wilder, Austrian-born American Academy
Award-winning director, speaking of actress Audrey Hepburn

Boobs, breasts, hooters, great rack—all these speak of a woman's ability to cause more accidents than all the airplane crashes in history.

Yep, we learned to use what we have to our advantage early in life. Just last week, Betty Sue caused a small pileup of cars right in front of Snoots Market. It was a sight to see, it even made the headlines in our local *Snoots Hollow Gazette.* Some said her figure was a work of art and she was not to be held responsible, others swore to the fact that only last year Betty Sue was flat as a pancake.

Heck, we all know the attention boobs get in the South. Aunt Nellie says her concern is keeping her breasts up where they belong. She says the best thing to do is sleep in a bra that keeps her beauties uplifted. You may find these at your local department stores or go online to barenecessities.com. Hollywood has been using sleep bras to keep their film stars looking perky for years.

The truth is that most women seem to think a bra fitter is not necessary and once they find a 32B in just the right color they tend to think things remain the same for them as the years pass. In case you missed this chapter, *things have moved.* Now is the time to work with a bra fitter to keep "the girls" in their properly fitted spot. You should see a bra fitter every two years, especially if you have lost or gained a bit of weight.

We have a secret in the South about small boobs, and it's one we never let anyone know about! You can fool most of our guys with just a little help from Snoots Market. If you thought oranges were just for juice, well, I am here to tell you that they can last up to four months tucked inside your bra, and they smell real sweet, too. One more trick for fooling the eye and simply looking better in your clothing: bras with "gel-filled" cups. These look so natural, they even move when you walk! Talk about looking real. . .just saying.

Body Care
Anything of beauty can dry up unless you take the time to keep a good moisture barrier between you and the sun. Aunt Nellie swears by lard as a skin cream. Me, I prefer the same idea with a twist: EVO, extra virgin oil, is my favorite and it has proven the test of time. Yes,

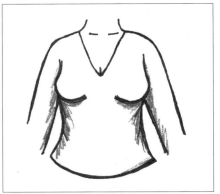

Droopy Boobs...lumps and bumps in need of emergency care

Perky Boobs – that's what I'm talking about!

you can use the oil you will find in the grocery store, but I like to get mine from the kitchen stores in the mall. They carry the small *sample sizes* and do buy the best extra virgin oil available.

Here's the best way to care for your face, breasts and décolleté.

• When you wash your face each evening, wash your chest as well. While the skin is still damp, rub some EVO on your face and your chest. Leave it on for about 45 minutes and then take it off with your hands. Then rub some on your legs, feet, and arms and sleep in it. Your skin will be shouting Hallelujah! by the next morning.

• A little contouring powder won't hurt, especially when used in just the right places. If God has not blessed you with big boobs, you can make your curves call out by choosing a powder a little darker than your skin. Use a good makeup brush, then apply a line between your breasts and blend well. This will create a shadow and look like the cleavage you did not know you had.

Of course, these are secret tips from the South and you will not tell a soul, right?

Southern Says...

JUDY

- Select a top that has three-quarter length sleeves—it hides what you don't want to show.
- Choose creams that tighten your arms. Perlier® is my favorite!
- Begin using the Buf-Puf®, a gentle abrasive sponge that gets rid of dead skin cells. Uncover your healthy skin!
- A little contouring on the turkey neck can do wonders. Don't over apply. Too much and the darker color will get stuck in the lines.

Spikey Says...

JUDY

- If you are a baby boomer and have not had a mammogram, go get one. Getting your boobs squished for a couple of minutes is a lot better than getting cancer.
- Avoid getting a black eye. Invest in a good workout bra to keep the girls still while jogging or working out.
- For hot days, try a little powder under the breasts. I love Anti-Monkey Butt® Anti-Friction Powder with calamine. The label alone will keep you laughing for weeks.
- Don't worry if you do not have the time to make an appointment for a good bra fitting. Essential Bodywear offers in-home consultations and fittings. Check them out at www.essentialbodywear.com.

Sassy Says...

JUDY

- Beautyblueprint.com rates Necksil® as the number one neck cream. This is an alternative to Ultherapy® or a neck lift. Buy it at necksil.com.
- Best toning for wavy arms. Push-ups. Do them and no cheating.
- Age spots and spider veins on décolleté are not to be on display. If you want to wear revealing necklines, better have them treated by a professional.
- Use a luminizing cream or powder on arms and collarbone for a youthful glow.

The Middle Third: Waist Not, Waist Full, Waist Away?

"I concentrate on exercises from the waist down, since that is the laziest part of a woman's body."
—Tina Louise, American actress

Just you wait! Just you wait! Your waist will gain weight! Here comes the fun part of middle years—middle age spread. There are two kinds of women: the X-ray and the womanly form. Then there is Christy Brinkley—she does not belong in this chapter.

X-ray women retain their thin, wiry figures but their faces look gaunt and show more wrinkles than the womanly types. The womanly type (which is most of us) gains weight in the torso and retains fat in the face. We womanly types can't figure out why our usual diet and exercise regimen is failing us. I'll tell you why. It's the e-word, estrogen, not to be confused with the f-word, fat.

As we go through menopause, our body's metabolic rate decreases along with our estrogen levels. We begin to lose fat in our arms, hips and legs, however that doesn't mean it gets flushed out. Oh no, that would be like winning the lottery on a two-dollar bet. Instead the fat we lose gets redistributed to our midsection, creating what I call *piano bench spread*. It's a stubborn kind of fat to shed and there's not much sympathy we get from doctors. "Just suck it up," they say. Oh yeah? How we are going to do that?

In this chapter, Southern Judy gets us all shook up as she once again dares us to stand in front of that mirror naked and stare at ourselves. The truth hurts, but let's just face the fact that *things have moved*. We need to know more than ever how to lift it, suck it and tuck it. You know Southern women are all about hospitality—but showing too much skin will only get you in the hospital, not on the hospitality committee. Southern says the best thing in our closet is a jacket and how it hides most everything there is to hide. She also advises against dressing too old and even worse, dressing too young.

Spikey has some great tips on how we can lose a bunch by lunch without consuming a box of laxatives. Her take on *accentuation avoidance* not only makes sense but makes us aware of a few clothing traps we've all fallen into. She has great advice on how to keep everything hoisted up, both in attitude and style. You will love her dress-to-deflect comments and cues.

As for me, I'll be sharing how you can truly *suck it up* with shape wear, or as they say in England, *lift and shift*. It's true, these innovations can make you look ten pounds thinner, shave a few inches off your piano bench middle, and improve your posture—something we need to work on no matter what we're wearing. When it comes to waistline patrol, I promise to keep you in the loop with the latest and best information. Stay in touch with us after reading this chapter. Just visit our website at www.3judys.com.

For most of us, our expanding waistline is the biggest challenge we experience as we age. Acceptance is one way to come to grips with a rounder circumference—and so is rejecting the *new* you. Somewhere in between lies a *happy middle* for you. Find out what makes you look trimmer without going for gastric bypass surgery, and how you can feel as gorgeous as a Rockette!

JUDY

Ladies,
Have Things Moved South?

By Southern Judy

"Everything slows down with age, except the time
it takes for cake and ice cream to reach your hips."
—John Wagner, British comics writer

Do you remember when we asked you to look into a three-way mirror, nude? Come on, you cannot dress in the dark for the rest of your life. I know, the truth hurts, but it is the only real "look" that can help you get up and do something that can turn your world around. We never stop wanting another chance: "One more time, Daddy," you would say as a child, as he pushed you higher and higher on the swing. Now today you want a do-over, another chance to prove you still have it.

When it comes to getting older, pretending does not work, trying too hard does not work, trying to dress like your teenager does not work.

The right bra works, the right underwear works, the right makeup works, the right hairstyle for your face works, and so does knowing when your clothing is too short or too tight or too low cut! Learning to accept what we have to work with works big time. Being you, only better, works every time.

We never said do not look your best; we just want you to know that there are rules that should be followed. Things have moved, so get a grip and hold onto your mirror, it's going to be a bumpy ride!

Unless you have had your head in the sand, you are aware that you have aged. We all have. There is no fountain of youth or miracle potion that makes age go away, yet we can postpone and fool the world for several years. You do not have to deal with back fat or rolls on the tummy, we have body shapers like Spanx® that come to our rescue. Unless you are working with a trainer, your butt has changed a bit, too. Now we have jeans that fit and make our butt look lifted and perked up. The dreaded "muffin top" can be controlled with a better-fitted waist in pants and skirts—this is where shapewear can help as well.

I know Marilyn Monroe said that a diamond is a girl's best friend, but I am here to tell you that a *jacket* is a girl's best friend! Jackets can hide a multitude of sins, including a little pooch in the tummy. If your legs are your best feature, keep your skirts to just above the knee or call attention to them by wearing tights or jeggings. Spend some money on a great pair of shoes that call attention to your long and beautiful legs.

Just this last week I overheard Aunt Nellie saying that in all her life she has not seen a better-looking and age-hiding person than Mary Lou. Most people in town do not even know when she was born.

Why, she would not even give her age when she married Jimmy Frank. Rumor has it she had her preacher hold his finger over the age part on the marriage certificate. Mary Lou simply does not show her age and we all wonder how she does it. Of course, if you get up early enough you might see her jogging around town and if you watch her at the church dinners she eats only salads. Come to think of it, we have never seen her at the dessert table, not once. Maybe we should copy her?

JUDY

With a Little Duct Tape and Spanx®
We Can Fix Any Body

By Sassy Judy

"Maybe it's true that life begins at fifty.
But everything else starts to wear out,
fall out, or spread out."
—Phyllis Diller, American actress and comedienne

Everything that once worked during my adult life—diet, exercise, body care—quit working during my forties faster than a fashionista could change clothes. I was eating less, exercising more and beginning to look like a bagel spread at a bar mitzvah. Princess-seamed dresses that once showed off my hourglass figure now made me look like a sausage stuffed in a too-small casing. I was obsessed with trying to figure out how to hide, conceal, camouflage, cover up and bury those hideous extra pounds.

Someone once said, "I have a shape. Round is a shape." Ok, how do I make that round shape into a figure eight? Nowadays it begins with a roll of industrial strength Spandex® and steel girders fit for a skyscraper—what we call shape wear. This is not a new idea. The desire for a tiny waist dates back to the 18th century when corsets were constructed from strategically placed whalebones to create an hourglass figure.

It worked back then, it still works today, and the construction is far more comfortable and breathable. If the trunk part of your figure is looking more like, well, a tree trunk, consider a waist cincher. The beauty of these garments is that they can trim up to four inches off your girth and promote better back support.

Many manufacturers make waist cinchers or shape bands. These fit from the hip line to under the bra line, are strapless—so you wear your own bra—and have adjustable hook and eye closures in the front.

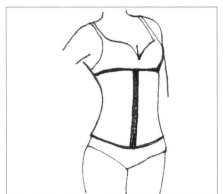
De-Tree Your Trunk in a Cinch!

Onesie – Convenient Control

Another alternative are slim vests or what I call "onesies." These are firm control panty shapers with a waistband that comes up just under the bra line. They smooth and shape the hips and waist and won't ride down because they have straps. Some "onesies" come with built in bras, other styles let you wear your own.

Grandma's old-time girdles are definitely a thing of the past. You can actually breathe and move in these new shape wear garments. The trick is to find a style that feels comfortable and still has the support you desire. Go to a lingerie store where you can get properly fitted and try on several styles. Once you get used to wearing shape wear you will even want to work out in it. For more detailed information on finding the perfect shape wear for you, I recommend visiting www.HourglassAngel.com.

At this stage of life, we have all heard every pulpit speech on the importance of exercise. I know many of us do pushups and squats, but when it comes to belly exercises the results are disappointing. Abdominal work won't eliminate belly fat, however it will improve back strength, posture and tone up the jiggle factor so you will look leaner. Pilates, Yoga and belly dancing all help tighten muscles and improve carriage—plus the boost in mental attitude, balance and coordination are all good things for boomer women.

Now let's tackle posture. Fact is, we slump. We slouch in our chairs, lean over our computers, and fail to walk the way our mothers told us to—head up, shoulders back, pelvis tucked—and she was right! All this body slack leads to sloped shoulders, curved backs and puffy tummies. In my opinion the only thing that should be puffy is my bank account and the Goodyear® blimp over the US Open®. Remember ladies, it is never too late to stand tall.

Finally, if you are one of those enviable, fit women who have a wee bit of extra belly fat, liposuction and a tummy tuck will probably make you happier than a summerhouse in the Hamptons. Consider it.

My personal struggle with midriff bulge is ongoing and I've got company. My mission is to search the latest advice on garments, fat blasters, detoxification programs and anything else that claims to whittle our waistlines. Just because we are boomers doesn't mean we can't have sexy curves. Visit me at www.3judys.com for up-to-date "waist away" information.

JUDY

Lose a Bunch by Lunch

By Spikey Judy

"I'm not overweight. I'm just nine inches too short."
—Shelley Winters, American actress

You bet I can lose a bunch by lunch. Just knock me out, suck it out and tuck it up. Unfortunately, I did not listen to my mother and married an engineer instead of a plastic surgeon, so I'm a few hundred thousand dollars away from my fantasy Franken-body. Mother Nature has taken our estrogen and replaced it with droopy boobs and potbellies. Short of going under the knife, how the heck do baby boomers deal with these unwelcome changes?

I'm here to tell you that there is a way to instantly look at least ten pounds thinner and it will not cost a fortune. What you wear, your posture and your overall attitude can shave pounds and years from your face and body.

Many women believe that the best way to hide the not-so-great bits is to drape themselves in miles and miles of loose, dark cloth. If no one can see our thickening waistline, then it cannot possibly exist. Let's not forget that black is slimming so make sure that those baggy pants and long tops are black or, if you want to live dangerously, choose dark grey. Looks better, huh? NOT! Just say no to loose, baggy, dark clothes. I call this "accentuation-avoidance"—covering everything to avoid accentuating the flaws. Instead, live dangerously, toss out those gunnysacks and play up your assets.

Thickening waistlines make us look a little like Sponge Bob Square Pants®. Wearing boxy tops is not the solution to square. Select tops that give the illusion of a waist, just don't cut straight across the stomach. Ruched tops are always a good choice. Ruching is a miracle; it adds soft gathering or pleats without adding bulk! Wrap tops can also provide a lovely hourglass look. Jackets and dresses with open collars add width to the shoulders. Choose tucked in waistlines that gently flare out from the middle. If your stomach is growing, but your butt and boobs are tiny, try a bloused top or dress. Make sure the garment has a wide enough elastic band and enough fabric to blouse above the waistline—this draws visual interest to the chest.

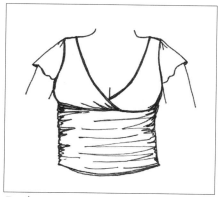

Don't Waste your Waistline — Ruch Instead

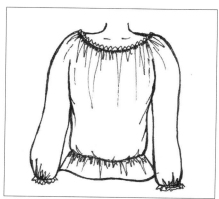

No Boobs? Try Blousing

Don't be afraid of color and accessories. Dress to deflect. In other words, draw the eye to your assets and away from the not-so-happy places. Get people to look at your face, not your waist. Choose jewelry that draws the eye toward your face. Reread Sassy Judy's chapter on makeup and play up those lips, eyes and cheekbones.

Finally, stand up straight and blast your self-confidence. Get up right now and look in a full-length mirror. Think about how getting old sucks, and how wrinkled and saggy you are. Say out loud, "woe is me." Notice how you slump over and how that makes everything move to the middle of your body. Not very flattering, is it? Now— stand up straight, put your hands on your hips and face yourself in the mirror and say, "Hello, sexy." Wow! You just lost twenty pounds.

Challenge yourself to toss out those baggy, dreary, cover-up clothes. Get your waistline back by dressing to accentuate. Confidently stand up, throw your shoulders back, put your hands on your hips and sling a new Kate Spade® bag over your shoulder. Not only will you lose a bunch by lunch, you might get a lot at night!

Southern Says...

JUDY

- Spanx too expensive? Try JC Penney® for a great body slimmer with built in bra.
- Take advantage of a body wrap before that big night, it will last for hours.
- Check your underwear, does it need to be replaced with a form-fitting body slimmer to hide lumps and bumps?
- How do your pants fit? Get rid of the Mom jeans, you'll subtract years from your hips and thighs.

Spikey Says...

JUDY

- Try to avoid foods that add to the middle. Beer and fatty foods will add fat to your waistline. Don't be fooled by foods that are labeled non-fat or low-fat. Get your sweets from fruit.
- Make sure you are doing your crunches and sit ups correctly. A Pilates instructor will teach you how to fully engage your abs.
- If you have a large belly, do not wear little, thin belts that cut straight across. Instead choose a wrap or ruched top.
- When wearing control top panty hose, make sure the waistband covers the entire belly.

Sassy Says...

JUDY

- Good posture and sucking in your belly will make you look ten pounds thinner.
- Find a modern day corset to keep your middle molded.
- Having trouble pulling up those onesies? Dust some baby powder on the inside and it will slide right up. Feels good next to the skin, too.
- Don't forget the power of water. Drink a full 12 ounces before meals and you won't eat as much.

The Lower Third: Hips, Biscuits and Thighs

"Cultivate your curves—they may be dangerous but they won't be avoided."
—Mae West, American actress

Oh goody. We are now at the favorite parts of every woman's body—the section below the waist and above the knees. We are definitely not referring to our whoopee spots, we're talking about our bountiful butts and thunderous thighs. In our twenties and thirties, we called ourselves curvy. As our curves start to sag and look lumpy, we just want to call a plastic surgeon. At one time you might have been blessed with a tight little tush and tiny thighs. Nevertheless, gravity still takes over, leaving you with a droopy derriere and string cheese thighs.

Don't despair. Remember you are in good company. There are over seventy million baby boomers out there dealing with the same issues and the three Judys are here to lend you support and not just support hose.

In this chapter, Southern Judy helps us pick out the best jeans for our behinds. We are never too old to wear denim, however we do need to pay special attention to fit as well as back pocket size and placement. Jeans from the juniors department might look great on a 14-year-old, however more mature women are better served with a well fitting jean designed specifically for the middle-aged body. Southern also gives us tips to lift and enhance formerly tight backsides.

Spikey Judy, that's me, will discuss those dreaded thighs, emphasizing the unfortunate onset of cellulite. I recommend the three T's—toning, tanning and treatment—to deal with lumpy legs. Then I will share some common sense clothing selections that can contain the flab and balance the leg shape with the rest of the body.

Sassy Judy helps us harness our hips by analyzing our hip lines. Do you have a high hip line like Marilyn or a low hip line like Beyonce? Depending on your shape and the location of your bounty, she recommends the best options for encasing your butt. The key here is to keep the body looking proportioned while playing up our best assets. She ends by giving us an easy, painless alternative to liposuction—the lunchtime lipo. Sign me up!

Don't spend the rest of your life sitting on your butt. Learn how to dress your hipline, tone your gams and reintroduce your backside to a good fitting pair of jeans. It's the last thing people see as you walk away, so make it a va-va-voom view.

JUDY

Go-go Hips.
Are You a High or a Low?

By Sassy Judy

"JLo turned it butt-style. Having a large-scale situation in the back was part of mainstream American beauty. Girls wanted butts now."
—Tina Fey, American actress, author, producer

I own plenty of real estate. It is well mounded and covers a large area. I'm speaking of my hips. The minute I eat a cracker it travels directly from my esophagus to my assets and settles in for a long cozy winter. Never one to have straight Twiggy hips, I've had to deal with my curvy cakes my entire life. I remember the days I lay flat on my back and used pliers to zip up my "nothing-comes-between-me-and-my-Calvin Kleins®" jeans. Thank goodness today we have Spandex® that allows the hinterland more room to roam. It's reassuring to know that while fashion still favors stick figures, celebs like JLo and Beyoncé give us reason to ride the curves. Even so, it's a balancing act to make clothing look proportioned when we're watching our rear view mirror.

Let's consider where your hip line hits. Stand in front of a mirror and notice where the fleshiest part of your hip is. Are you meatier just slightly below your waistline? If so, you have a high hip line much like Marilyn Monroe. What this means is you will want to avoid pleats, folds, darts, gathers and pumpkin-sized pockets at the bottom of your jackets. In other words, avoid bulk at your broadest point. Your best choices are straight, flat fronts, bootleg or straight-leg pants. Also, forget about printing! Not even that famous four-letter word, *Pink,* on your backside is allowed. The same goes for pockets on jeans—too much acreage, dahlings. Stick to shapes that drape smoothly over your curves for a flattering, more slimming silhouette.

The next hip line to look at is the low hip line. Are you fairly narrow below the waist and carry the meatiest flesh close to your thighs? You have a low hip line and will very possibly have saddlebags—a lovely descriptive word! Low hip line ladies want to avoid anything tight across the beam and choose A-line or flared shapes. Often called the pear shape or triangle, these low-lying hipsters look best when not on full display. Wear pants that fall straight from the waist and have plenty of ease in the seat. Don't bother with molded jeans or tight pants unless you want to attract attention to your playing field. Keep those cheeks in check.

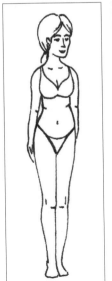 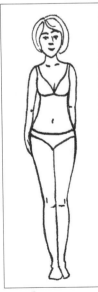

High hips were Marilyn's Assets!

Low hips are Beyonce's Booty!

Here's some good and bad news about getting older: As we go through menopause our hips actually slim down a bit. As estrogen levels drop, weight stops going to our hips and instead goes to our mid section—hence the *meno-pot.* If it's not one place it's another.

Now let's talk about go-go hips! We all know about liposuction and have heard horror stories of lipo gone wrong. What we really want is a way to get body contouring without sucking out the fat with a hose. Enter Lunchtime Lipo! This is a laser treatment guaranteed to melt away muffin tops, mid-section excess fat, and annoying fat on our hips and thighs. The best candidates have a healthy lifestyle, exercise regularly and are close to their ideal weight. The sessions take about forty minutes each and it takes about six sessions to get the results you're looking for. With Lunchtime Lipo, you can lose nearly four inches of extra fat and feel fit and sculpted. This is my birthday wish.

Not sure whether you have a low hip line or high hip line? Send us a photo on our www.3judys.com website and we'll tell you what you've got and how to get it dressed!

JUDY

Why, Oh Why These Thighs?

By Spikey Judy

"I have flabby thighs, but fortunately my stomach covers them."
—Joan Rivers, American comedienne and entrepreneur

I have always had larger than life thighs. Give me a hammer and I could be Thorina, goddess of thunder thighs. Weight gain pumped up my legs with cottage cheese, definitely the large curd variety, and weight loss resulted in stringy cheese. Goodbye shorts and bathing suit bottoms, hello industrial grade support hose.

Very few women are satisfied with the size and appearance of their thighs. Thin or fat, most baby boomer women are plagued with cellulite. Cellulite is caused by fat pressing up against the skin while the cords of connective tissue pull down. Sadly, there is no permanent cure for cellulite. You can have it sucked out, but it will eventually come back. The best option is to minimize the appearance of cellulite through the three T's: toning, tanning and treatment.

Toning is best achieved through exercise targeted at the problem areas. Make sure to consult a doctor before starting any exercise program. Also, spend the money and invest in a few personal trainer sessions at a local gym. A trainer will help you put together a fitness program that fits your lifestyle and also makes sure you are performing the exercises for optimal benefit. Most aerobic exercise—walking, running, swimming or biking—will help tighten the leg muscles so that the connective tissue can win the tug-of-war with the fat. Squats, with or without lighter hand weights, will further tone legs and butt.

Tanned skin can camouflage unsightly legs. That said, do not start sunbathing. The damage caused by the sun will add age a lost faster than lumpy legs. Instead, consider using a self-tanner or investing in a spray tan. Before any self-tanning applications, make sure your legs are clean and thoroughly exfoliated. Spray tanning is preferable to the do-it-yourself method because it leaves you with better, more even coverage.

Treating the cellulite can be done at home or by a medical professional. Topical creams, which contain caffeine, dehydrate the fat and make the skin look smoother. This is a short-term, inexpensive option.

Dermatologists can use needles to loosen the connective tissue and break up the unsightly dents, or melt the fat using lasers. Costs for this office procedure usually range from $1,000 to $4,000. A thigh lift is an option if you have very saggy, wrinkly thighs. This is a major surgical procedure that involves incisions in the groin area—yikes! Consult with a Board Certified Plastic Surgeon if you are considering having this done.

Another quick fix is to wear clothing that complements your thighs. Darker hose with some support creates a taut look that hides cellulite. Don't wear pants that are tight around the thighs and taper down to the ankle. Instead, wear a boot cut pant that flares slightly at the ankles. This will balance out the leg. Save busier patterns for the upper half of the body. Also, wear tops that either stop at your waist or below your thighs. A lovely duster with a cinched-in waist that flares over the hips and thighs will take away inches and cover up lumps.

Toning, tanning, and treatments combined with wise wardrobe selections will give you a leg up to turn those cheesy, thunder thighs into great gams. Give it a try—bathing suit season is always closer than you think!

JUDY

Do These Jeans Make My Butt Look Big?

By Southern Judy

"Ummm, I think my butt looks too big in these jeans."
—Kim Kardashian, American TV star and clothing designer

In all our inventions and efforts at staying fashion-forward, we are still in search of the perfect garment that allows us to have the tiniest looking waist and a curvy, lifted butt. Is that asking too much? Butt, bum, tight end, junk in the trunk, I still think they got those phrases from us and our never-ending quest for a good looking rear view.

The Gold Rush of the 1850s changed the way people dressed. Why, when that first pair of waist coveralls was stitched by Mr. Levi Strauss himself, you could hear Aunt Nellie's great-great-grandmother sing Hallelujah! From the moment coarse canvas switched to brushed twill, women have spent more years trying on jeans than raising children.

Can I say, finding that perfect pair of jeans is about as fun as buying a two-piece bathing suit? Jeans can make or break a good-looking lower body. The right pair will smooth the hips, ease over bulky thighs and create an illusion of long-legged beauty. Those fashion designers leave nothing to chance. They even research the proper shape, placement and detail for those back pockets. Just a smidgen off can make our butt look too big or heaven forbid, flat as a pancake.

The right pair of jeans is worth every penny, yes, but let's talk a moment about what that right pair is if you are over forty. Jeans come and go and so does our allegiance to the best of the best in denim paradise. You can almost hear the angels sing as we put on the sucked-in-waist, butt-

Yes, I can, yes I can...still look good in my jeans

lifted, pockets-placed-just-right pair. If we can get them zipped, we will hand over all our hard earned pay willingly and with a smile of gratitude.

Sneaking into your daughter's closet and stealing her jeans or her "label" is not for you. Who are you trying to fool? It only makes you look older, besides it embarrasses your kids! There is a difference—your body is not the same anymore. I am not saying you cannot look great, because the three Judys are here for you, just lose the "hot and sexy" from your vocabulary.

You have seen how women look when they are past the age of wearing the long hairstyle, low-cut jeans and too much makeup: it is just sad. That same woman should be sporting an updated hairstyle and rocking the most long-lasting, best-fitting, body-trimming pair of Diane Gilman® jeans she can find on Home Shopping Network®. *This* woman is a baby boomer who understands that her body has changed and she, like all of you, wants the same thing—to *look darn good in those jeans!*

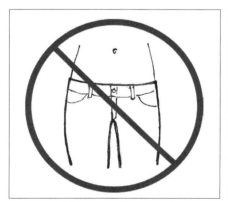

Teen Jeans fit ONLY teen bodies! Don't even think about it

The "I don't care how I look" MOM Jeans

Age appropriate does not mean you are not sexy. Choose wisely for your true body style, and you can still cause a car crash in *your* new jeans, if you know what I mean.

Now, just in case you wondered what Aunt Nellie had to say about making our butts look good, according to her and Mrs. Anderson they were born with—or may I say blessed with—an uplifted, tucked-tight derriere. To our shock, Mr. Sam Evans overheard them talking about it, and he said that's the God's honest truth about both Aunt Nellie and Mrs. Anderson. Why those two gals just blushed and remarked he must have lost his mind in his old age—and you know they said that with just the cutest wink.

If you want your ends to justify the jeans, consider this:
• Alterations are not just for fancy pants. With an expert nip and tuck here and there, any pant will look its best on *your* body. That includes jeggings, skinny legs and boot cut styles of jeans. Most dry cleaners offer a tailoring service.

Southern Says...

JUDY

- Diane Gilman Jeans fit in all the right places and hides inches. Buy them on HSN.
- Same color head to toe makes you look slimmer. We call it the monochromatic look.
- A jacket is your best friend. It hides a tummy or hips.
- Exercise and diet are key to getting a tight tush. If you're in a hurry, or believe that Southern gals don't sweat, buy a slip-on panty that has extra padding on the seat. These will uplift your bum instantly. Check out your nicer lingerie department.

Spikey Says...

JUDY

- Lunges are a great exercise for the hips. If you have sore or weak knees, try doing lunges in the shallow end of a swimming pool. The water will offer additional resistance.
- Stay out of the boy's and men's departments. There is no such thing as unisex jeans for women over fifty.
- If you have issues with cellulite or saggy belly syndrome you may want to consider Velashape®. Consult with a qualified practitioner.

Sassy Says...

JUDY

- If your assets cover broad territories, wear dark colors from the waist down. Wear brighter, lighter colors from the waist up.
- Always wear dark denim jeans to look proportioned.
- Hips broader than your shoulders? Add a soft shoulder pad to fill out the shoulder area—instant body balance!
- Boot-leg, slight-flared or full-flared pants keep biscuits from looking like buns.

Legs, Leggings or Coveralls?

Dorothy: "Oh c'mon Blanche, age is just a state of mind!"
Blanche: "Tell that to my thighs."
—Golden Girls, TV show, 1985

Just a stroll around the block can give you some insight on our legs and how we use or abuse them. We all have been given the same amount of time in each day, yet some of us choose to allow time to take over our bodies. It is not helping us stay trim if we just sit and watch as the world goes by. Getting out there is all it takes to keep a check on how our legs look and how they serve us.

Yet here I sit with my coffee cup looking at the world beyond my window and thinking maybe tomorrow morning will be the first day I walk around the block. There are lots of excuses I could and do use: *It looks like rain,* or *That sun will bleach out my latest hair color,* or a hundred other useless reasons for not getting out there and walking. Do I know that walking, jogging or running will help improve the look of my legs? In a word, absolutely!

In this chapter, Spikey Judy reminds us our calves are sometimes an inherited trait that can be traced back for several generations. She offers tips for glamorizing those less-than-perfect gams. Next, Sassy Judy says wearing pants or a longer skirt will hide your less-than-toned ankles and legs. She offers specific advice on covering up to look your best.

While it's true hiding the ankles and calves under layers of fabric may solve your concerns, wearing your skirts too long adds age to any outfit. Keeping your skirts to your knee or just above creates a younger look and will make you feel better about the flaws you're trying to hide.

Lots of imperfections can be hidden by leg makeup. One of the best is by Joan Rivers called *Right to Bare Legs*®. Many of my clients swear by its coverage and sheer appearance. Spikey Judy also has her own preference and advice for covering flaws.

As for clothes, I am not telling you to go into your daughters' closet and wear her mini skirt. The simple A-line or even a pencil skirt is still within the baby boomers' goal to dress great for every season.

Aunt Nellie says we are making too much of this leg thing, well I don't know about that. Why, just yesterday at church Louise Mae looked strange and we could not decide what she had done to herself. I am not one to talk, but she was orange all over her legs, and her body as well. A person cannot keep that to themselves, you know.

After Henry, Louise Mae's husband, died, God rest his soul, she seemed to go to the mall a lot more than usual. She came to church last week with a pink cast to her silver hair and we all just smiled and thought how she had really lost it. This week coming in looking all orange was more than we could take. After services, Aunt Nellie walked right up to her and asked what she had done to herself. Louise

Mae told her it was a spray tan to cover her spider veins and her white legs, and that Amber, a cute teen working part time at Bertha's Tan Tower, told her it would last two weeks.

You might have heard that the legs are the last to go, now I think we should keep them looking good for as long as possible. That means as sure as the sun comes up tomorrow I will begin to walk and do Spikey's exercises to keep my legs looking good...if it doesn't look like rain.

JUDY

Knees that Need a Mention

By Southern Judy

"Ankles are nearly always neat and good looking, but knees are nearly always not."
—Dwight D. Eisenhower, 34th President of the United States

Watching my mother on her knees teaching me to tie my shoes is a sweet memory forever etched in my mind. Knees seen in any other way is just not a pretty sight. Oh, I am not saying that my babies' knees were not the cutest things, but as we get older the cute goes away...way away. Weight gain or weight loss plays havoc with an already tender subject as we age. The truth is most women do not like their knees, and they will hide them at all cost.

When we were in our twenties, wearing a mini skirt was not a problem. Thinking back I am not really sure I had knees or at least I do not remember them as a concern. Now knees seem to be an issue when choosing what to wear, especially when it is mostly for a special occasion. It is a real concern when it's your class reunion and you've run into your old boyfriend. Now that's what I call a serious situation.

Skin is skin and it all needs attention to look and feel its best. Moisture in our skin seems to go away and dry skin takes its place. That's one complaint we have as baby boomers.

The best creams are the ones that hold in that precious moisture. Perlier® makes one of the most effective body creams we have found. It's called *Body Honey Miel* and is known for its anti-aging natural ingredients. Clients tell me they would not go a day without it. As for me, I have it automatically shipped once a month. This product does most of its magic after you exfoliate first. Then add this luxurious body balm to your knees.

Not everyone feels as I do about special-order products. If it doesn't come in a jar from Pete's Stop-N-Go then Aunt Nellie refuses to buy or try any new treatment for her skin. "God only knows what is in the stuff they sell today," she says, and she may have a point. Have you read the labels lately? All those words we cannot pronounce! We have no idea what those ingredients do to our bodies and it's scary.

Aunt Nellie recalls, "Last time Sarah Jean tried one of those new creams we heard that her face was so swollen that it scared her cat. We have not seen hide nor hair of Precious since."

Thinking back on last week, while we were sitting on the porch drinking some peach tea, I began to look at the women who were visiting. There was not a deep wrinkle on any of them. Fact is that most of them could pass for women much younger than those the same age in town. Could it be that fresh air and some of Pete's Stop-N-Go wonder creams really work or is it something in the tea?

JUDY

Calves that Need a Milking

By Spikey Judy

"Darling, the legs aren't so beautiful,
I just know what to do with them."
—Marlene Dietrich, German-American actress and singer

Thickening calves or skinny chicken legs, bulging blue veins or lackluster skin make baby boomer women want to hide their legs. Now that we are older, does that mean we are relegated to wearing granny skirts and knee-highs? No. You can dare to bare—a little leg that is.

Thick calves are often inherited. If genetics have given you the short, thick end of the peg leg, don't worry. There are ways to visually minimize gargantuan gams.

The first rule is never, ever wear pants or skirts that stop at the thickest part of the calf. A horizontal line is like a flashing arrow. It

Warning! Wide Load Leggings

Stretchy Boots – Cure All for Thick Calves

calls attention to whatever is being crossed. Capri pants are a definite no-no. Not only will the calf look bigger, but the whole leg appears shorter, throwing your silhouette off balance. Instead, choose a longer cut pant.

The same rule applies to skirts, although it gets trickier here. Wear a hemline that stops just below the thickest part of the calf. Pair the skirt with a pair of stretchy pull on boots. The hemline of the skirt should cover the top part of the boot. Alternatively, dark hose and a pair of high heels will also slim the leg. If you are averse to stilettos or unable to wear higher heels, try platform wedge shoes. These will add height while keeping the foot more parallel to the ground. For summer, get a spray tan so you can wear a sexy pair of sandals with a skirt or dress. Again, if you have thicker calves, avoid shoes that have ties that go up the leg like gladiator sandals.

If you have chicken legs, for goodness sakes get up off your chair and put some muscle on those calves. Calf raises are the best way to tone the lower legs. These exercises can be done standing or sitting so you don't have to get up off your chair! For sitting calf raises, perch on the edge of a sturdy chair or weight bench. Place a weight bar on your knees and slowly raise and lower your heels off the ground without lifting your toes.

Standing calf raises can be done on a flat surface, on the edge of a stair, or with your heels hanging off the edge of a board. Hold hand-held weights while you raise and lower both your heels. Alternate by raising one heel, then the other. Be sure to stand straight while you perform this exercise.

Finally, swimming is fantastic for toning legs. The water offers resistance and is low impact, which will prevent added strain to the legs. As always, be sure to consult your doctor before you start any exercise program.

Fat or skinny, most aging legs become infested with spider veins. These are unsightly and harmless. They don't affect your circulation and are not a sign of an impending stroke. Rather than calling the exterminator, unless his legs are uglier than yours, go see a doctor and get rid of them! The standard treatment is called scleropathy. The doctor injects a solution directly into the spider veins. This kills the spirally offenders and then the body reabsorbs them. Scleropathy is a fairly affordable, not-as-painful-as-it-sounds procedure. It's an effective cure that lasts longer if you wear support stockings post-procedure.

Tanning or leg makeup will provide coverage until scleropathy does its job. Sally Hansen makes a wonderful leg makeup that goes on smoothly, provides excellent coverage and, unlike most self-tanners, does not smell weird. Do shave and exfoliate before you use makeup or tanners. Otherwise, you might end up looking like an aging tiger.

As with the thighs, toning, tanning and treatment will improve the appearance of your calves. Smart wardrobe selections also make a world of difference. Take the moo and cluck out of those calves and put the ooh-la-la back in.

JUDY

Ankles that Cankle in the Night

By Sassy Judy

"I have a microphone on one ankle and an ankle bracelet on the other, so I'm well balanced today."
—Martha Stewart, American lifestyle doyenne

Can you believe it was barely over a hundred years ago that women dared not bare their ankles? The first peek of an ankle was during the early 1900s. Gone were the sweeping skirts of the 1800s, and whoa— when skirt lengths became shorter, ankles were exposed. Today, this would be like not wearing panties under a skirt. What dangerous doings those times were!

If you are one of the lucky owners of shapely, nicely tapered ankles, then you know wearing pants, skirts, dresses, shoes and boots is friendly territory. You have no issue wearing capris, gladiator sandals or lace-up shoes. Your calves and ankles are well-proportioned and attractive. This chapter is not for you. Right now I'm talking to those women who have cankles—a genetic condition where the ankle and calf look like they are one piece, like a block of wood. In other words, you have fat ankles.

Now this is a condition I hardly think any of us should obsess over. However, there are gyms that actually target this area with specially designed workouts called *say no to cankles*. Honestly, if exercise helped don't you think there would have been a cankle revolution the minute women started raising their hemlines?

We're talking fat here, and it's a matter of being born this way. Yes, some plastic surgeons are performing liposuction to reduce fat deposits. Still, the calf and ankle can't be sculpted the way thighs can.

So what's there to do about cankles? Dress them down, dress them up, let them be and you'll have luck! Here are a few style pointers to keep all eyes off your cankle district.

• **Befriend your pants.** Wear them long, straight leg or loose. Keep the colors neutral or dark. Skip the skinny jeans and leggings. The point is to elongate your leg and draw attention away from your knees on down.

Old Lady Skirt – Should be the No Lady Skirt!

• **Wear fabulous tops.** Elizabeth Taylor never had lovely legs but she certainly had lovely eyes. Keep the visual interest around your face.

• **No old lady skirts.** Too many women with cankles wear dumpy looking long skirts that make them look old. Instead try a maxi dress. Now that looks hot! If you want to wear a dress or skirt, keep the show dark from the knee down. That means choose dark, opaque stockings and pair them with dark shoes. Your shoes and stockings should match the hemline, not contrast it.

• **Shoes and boots.** Wear shoes with a rounded or square toe and chunkier heel. The trick is to balance the wide part of your ankle. Stilettos will make you look like you are balancing a refrigerator on a pair of toothpicks. Wear boots that come up to the knee and feel comfortable over the calf.

Seriously, nothing much can be done about cankles. With a little style savvy, you can move them away from the check out zone and into the safety zone. At our age, let's focus on the face!

Southern Says... JUDY

- White legs are bad at any age, Joan Rivers' Right to Bare Legs® cream is great!
- Have fun with your A-Line skirt. Wear it just above the knees.
- Remember to care for your legs with a good, rich lotion every day.
- If it's skin, keep the moisture in. Even household products work such as olive oil and Vaseline®.

Spikey Says... JUDY

- Just say no to knee socks with skirts or shorts. They're only cute on ten-year-olds and strippers trying to look like ten-year-olds.
- A lot of stress goes into the knee joints, so consider supplements. I give my retired race horse glucosamine and he can still go over a jump! Guess what? They make glucosamine for humans as well.
- Anklets are great if you have sexy ankles. They do not make thick ankles look sexier.
- Be sure to exfoliate your legs and knees. It leaves the skin silky smooth.

Sassy Says... JUDY

- The legs are the last to go—if you got 'em, flaunt 'em!
- Showing off your legs means you either wear hosiery, leg makeup or have those nasty spider veins removed. Just because your legs are shapely doesn't mean they don't show their age in other ways.
- Thinking of leggings? Check out the rear view mirror before you wear them in public.
- A terrific pair of dark leggings, boots and a long, fitted jacket can peel away ten years off an old style.

Dr. Feel Good Feet

"My shoes are special shoes for discerning feet."
—Manolo Blahnik, Spanish shoe designer extraordinaire

There is something about a girl and her shoes (it could be the glass slipper syndrome) and darn if we aren't all a little guilty of buying a pair of shoes that is just closet jewelry—for admiration only. That's okay, because history supports our shoe passion. For five hundred years, high heels have been a measurement of status, stature and sex appeal. Occasionally there have been fashion lapses to embrace low-heeled shoes but for the most part, high heels have dominated women's preferences, until recently.

As we get older, our feet can grow an additional half-size or more. Couple that with a decline in foot health, plus the rise of savvy designers, and we now have more shoes to buy than sandwiches in a deli. Modern shoes can be stylish *and* easy on the feet. Thanks to those same high-end designers, we can also spend a year's paycheck on one pair of shoes. Oh, if only to win the lottery!

Truthfully, shoes make or break an outfit. That's why we're about to tell you how to balance beauty and the bunions.

In New York, we see women trading pumps for sneakers to negotiate bumpy sidewalks and subway lines. They even change shoes in the middle of the street if necessary. Other women are more fashion-conscious; they change from pumps to cute flats. Frankly, every woman should be swapping out heels for flats and keep the sneakers for workouts. Heels to sneakers? That is so last century.

As you can see, not everyone is head over heels about heels or willing to endure pain because it's pretty—as someone I know does. Not everyone believes that someone wearing *sensible* shoes should be stored in a morgue—as someone I know does. Not everyone has to agree that shoes should be as high as a skyscraper—as someone I know does. What if you don't agree with that someone I know and insist on wearing foot soothing, comfort shoes?

In the coming pages, Southern Judy tells us what *not* to wear. You'll learn what's up-to-date, not out to pasture. She also explains how old lady shoes can make you look older than what's left in the bargain bin at Pete's Stop-N-Go. Then she'll share her thoughts on shoes being both comfortable and practical and will put her down-home spin on those old, *you've got to be kidding,* clodhoppers.

Spikey Judy shuffles forward with her chapter on foot crises and how to deal with chronic pain. From bunions to bone spurs she confronts how to solve foot problems and save our feet from hurting so much. We take nearly ten thousand steps per day, so foot pain needs to be at low tide. She reviews proper foot care, when to see a podiatrist, how often we should have a pedicure and the importance of foot exercises.

She even includes some simple examples that will strengthen and improve our flexibility and stability.

And I, Sassy Judy, will tell you how to pick the prettiest pair of high heels that have style *and* relative comfort. Notice the emphasis on "relative."

Of all the steps we can take, having a *Dancing with the Stars* attitude is the most important. Beware that Crocs® croak! If you can hose off your shoes along with your patio furniture they don't belong on your feet. Save the Birkenstocks®, loafers, sneakers and Doc Martins® for the farm or the gym.

Do you think diamonds are a girl's best friend? Think again. Peep toes, or platforms, or sky-high stilettos, Manolos® are a girl's best friend!

JUDY

Who Can Stand Those Old Lady Shoes (OLS)?

By Southern Judy

"I still have my feet on the ground, I just wear better shoes."
—Oprah Winfrey, American TV personality and actress

Somewhere between all the shoes I can hide and the ones I like to wear and the others I love to show off is a husband screaming, "Enough already!"

You just cannot stop a girl in a great pair of shoes. Her shoes will tell you if she has made it to the top or is still on her way. Shoes seem to speak their own language and boy, do they have a hold on style. It is almost magic when a girl spots just the right shoe, her eyes lock and her credit card starts to float out of her purse as if it knows when to come to attention.

Some say it is love at first sight, others say it goes back to playtime in Mama's closet, but there is definitely a connection between a girl and her shoes. Designers have fun playing with our affections. Just when we think we have found the shoe of a lifetime, they change the styles just to keep us on our toes.

Shoes, like styles, come and go throughout our lifetime. Some stay for a while like special shoes—our first pair of heels or our wedding shoes. I have a pair that just look good in my studio. They are a six-inch platform, decorated with a wild animal print. These are sitting on my desk right now. They've never been worn, and they never will be. They are just eye candy for me.

There is a serious side of shoes that we need to talk about ladies, so listen up. It is not really about hoarding shoes; it's just the opposite. I'm talking about never changing the style, or for that matter the shoe! You have seen shoes like these on some women you know, styles that have no right to be worn anymore. Those women will tell you how much they paid for those shoes and that they still look good on and one more thing, let's say it together, "They are comfortable."

Please, for the sake of women who see you in these shoes, get another style and give these a decent burial! They are not pretty, they came over in the Ark, and they scream, "I am old."

You are too young for that Velcro® strap across your foot, too young for that lace-up shoe, too young for that pair you've been wearing for the last ten years!

Let me tell you a secret. Aunt Nellie had to sneak into Mary Beth's closet and that was not easy with the slick vinyl brick pattern on her floor. Thankfully Mary Beth was hard of hearing. It was something Aunt Nellie had to do, she says, because she just could not take it any longer. I am not one to talk, but God knows those ruby red sparkling shoes Mary Beth got on sale at Pete's Stop-N-Go in 1946 had to go. Fact is, at the last meeting of the Valley View Quilting Club the girls decided to draw straws to see who'd swipe the shoes. Seems like Aunt Nellie got the short straw.

Don't be like Mary Beth. Here are my tips for updating your footwear.

- **Purge, then binge.** What is in your shoe closet that needs to be updated? Really keep an open mind when getting rid of those "used to be" favorites. Ask a friend to come over and help, listen to her opinion. Once you clean out your closet, you can binge on a few new favorites.
- **Put it in neutral.** Choosing a neutral color shoe will allow you to wear it longer. Quality is really important here.
- **Protect your precious pair.** Buy an inexpensive pair of shoes that look just like your quality shoes. Wear those on a rainy day and save your good pair for fairer weather.

JUDY

Get Up, Stand Up and Dance Your Feet Off!

By Spikey Judy

"My mother told me I was dancing before I was born. She could feel my toes tapping wildly inside her for months."
—Ginger Rogers, American actress and dancer

Remember Steve Martin and his "happy feet" routine in the late 1970s? His feet would begin to dance out of control. Thirty years ago, we could put on a pair of sexy heels and dance the night away. Now, baby boomers are living with the consequences of overly happy feet. Bunions, fallen arches, bone spurs and funky toes are pretty depressing signs of age. Ugly orthopedic shoes are taking the place of sexy stilettos. Nowadays, sitting at home, feet up and watching *Dancing with the Stars* on television is the closest we're getting to cutting a rug.

Not me! I am going to keep dancing until the day I move on to the giant discothèque in the sky. You, too, can put the joy back into your aging feet. Clinical care, foot exercises and a good pedicure will tickle your toes and get you back out on the dance floor.

If your feet are starting to resemble the clawed toes of a T-Rex, it might be time to make an appointment with a podiatrist. The average person takes 8,000 to 10,000 steps per day. Over time, toes get squished, arches break down and bone spurs form. A podiatrist will be able to diagnose foot problems and prescribe appropriate treatment. In severe cases, surgery might be required. If problems are caught early enough, less invasive remedies, such as shoe inserts, are available. The doctor might suggest you wear different shoes, but never fear: many inserts can be worn in a favorite pair of shoes. There are plenty of comfort shoes that won't make you look like an old lady, so you will not need to sacrifice fashion for foot care.

It is never too late to start a good foot exercise program. Exercise will strengthen and add flexibility, which will help prevent or improve unsightly feet. The American Academy of Orthopedic Surgeon's (AAOS) website www.aaos.org provides a free download of a foot and ankle conditioning program. All of the exercises can be performed at home. A couple of examples include:

- **Golf Ball Roll.** Sit on a chair with both feet planted securely on the floor. Roll a golf ball under each arch for about two minutes. Your feet will be singing the *Hallelujah Chorus*.
- **Towel Curls.** Again, sit on a chair with both feet on the floor. I love exercises that can be done while sitting! Place a small towel in front of your feet. Grab the towel with your toes and curl it toward you. Relax and repeat ten times.

Make sure to warm up before starting the exercises. AAOS recommends five to ten minutes of low impact activity like walking. Do stretching exercises like the Golf Ball Roll before strengthening routines like Towel Curls. If you feel any pain while performing the exercises, stop and consult a physician.

Lastly, set aside the time to get a full service pedicure at least once or twice per month. A good pedicure includes more than just nail care.

The entire foot and usually ankles are treated in a warm water bath and massage. If needed, a pumice stone is used on the dry, callused portions of the foot. I also recommend investing in a more thorough foot massage at least four times per year. There are numerous nerve endings in the feet and a good foot massage is an orgasmic experience!

Take care of your feet. It's time to retire the bunny slippers, slip on your favorite party shoes and dance, dance, dance.

JUDY

Yes, You Can Stand in Those Stilettos!

By Sassy Judy

"I don't know who invented high heels,
but all women owe him a lot."
—Marilyn Monroe, American actress

I admit it, I am a shoe-aholic. Nothing excites me more than a new pair of killer heels. I mean the kind with the six-inch stilettos and pointy toes. The kind you can't walk in and are considered brave—some say ridiculous—just for putting them on. People ask me constantly, "How do you walk in those heels? My answer, "Carefully, very carefully."

How much do I like high heels? Let's say my pedicurist has made a healthy profit over the years dealing with my penchant for spikes and

Live Dangerously. Step out in Stiletto Style!

height. I don't need to be taller I just love the way high heels elongate my legs and streamline my figure. Wearing sky-high stilettos is my big secret for instant weight loss; it's like losing a bunch by lunch.

I know I'm an exception to most of us boomers who want comfort over challenge. One woman once told me her shoes had to be "accommodating." C'mon. Your shoes don't have to obey commands, they just need to fit comfortably and look good with your clothes. It's also true you can wear a higher heel than you think. All it takes is an open mind and a willing foot.

The classic pump in the right size and heel height can update your wardrobe in a nanosecond. Please don't resist a bit of a platform either. Platforms provide an extra layer of sole that makes the shoe more comfortable. If you have foot issues, look for styles that are more open. There is also a style called D'orsay, that has cutouts on the sides. Support your toe and heel with additional cushioning if necessary, there are inserts designed to do just this. It's also crucial to practice walking in high heels. Put them on at home and break them in. Here's a dare. Try walking naughty, real naughty! I once had a dance instructor spend an entire hour teaching me how to walk in stilettos like a high-class call girl. What fun that was. I learned a trick or two about the stiletto strut that I still use today when I want to make a diva entrance.

Can't walk in pumps? Dump the pumps. You can always find smart looking Mary Janes with the strap across the foot. These come in several heel heights and because of the strap, they provide more foot support. Here's something to consider about sling backs or strappy sandals. If your foot is broad at the toe and narrow at the heel, you have to be careful of the flip flop factor. No one wants to hear you come clacking and flapping down the hall, so be careful of the fit. Shoes should be seen, not heard.

Give the Old Lady Shoes the Boot!

Keep your shoes up to date. It is said we judge other people by their haircut and their shoes. I actually did a mini survey of this theory as I watched planeloads of people descend an escalator at JFK International Airport. All the old ladies were wearing frumpy, dumpy sneakers and tracksuits. Businesswomen wore sensible but stylish pumps and then there was that "fashion coma crowd" in which comes the horror show—the ones who wear their PJs with white socks and flip-flops.

Ladies, kick up your heels and give those old lady shoes the boot. Try some fun colors and explore heel heights that make you feel like the Eiffel Tower. Wear a pair of lacquer red shoes and match your lipstick to your shoes! You will have the most fun at your own one-woman show! After all, a much admired New York fashionista once said, "Darlings, dress for the theatre of your life." Now that's high-stepping style advice!

Southern Says...

 JUDY

- Models wear shoes a half size bigger for a busy day on their feet.
- Plus-size girls need a thicker heel, it balances the body.
- Pamper those feet with a great pedicure at least once a month.
- Don't let your shoes give your age away.

Spikey Says...

 JUDY

- Give reflexology a try. Applying pressure to these areas can help alleviate stress and open the flow of energy. Some swear by it!
- Don't have time for a good foot massage? You can buy a foot roller for less than $10. Roll your feet on it while reading or watching television.
- Don't be too matchy-matchy. Use shoes to add a pop of color to your wardrobe.
- Add a little peppermint essential oil into your body lotion to pep up tired feet.

Sassy Says...

 JUDY

- Shoes can be functional and fashionable. If you don't think so, carry two pair. There is even the perfect "changing shoes" bag from tinasloan@gmail.com
- For those who are severely foot impaired, ask about having butt fat transferred into the pads of your feet. This could be the ultimate two for one!
- Mother said my eyes and feet are the most important body parts to care for. Both are worthy of creams, or more, it depends on you. A little toe cleavage is a sexy little tease. Work it, ladies!

Hands of
Hope

"Old age is when the liver spots
show through your gloves."
—Phyllis Diller, American comedienne and actress

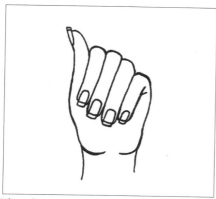

Thumbs Up to Getting Older!

One way to guess someone's age is to look at their hands. As we age, the moisture and fat flee from our hands, leaving us with dry, liver-spotted wrinkly claws. Let's not forget that because of protruding veins, hands begin to take on a sickly blue tone. Aging and repetitive motion can also bring on painful arthritis and carpal tunnel syndrome, which can further disfigure our hands. This is not fair! We're baby boomers and we've paid our dues. We deserve that giant diamond ring, even if we can't figure out how to get it to fit over our ever-expanding knuckles.

Unfortunately, we cannot wear gloves 24-hours per day—well we can, but it might look weird. Even if we reinstated the old trend of wearing one glove, what are we going to do with our other hand? Don't throw your hands up in despair. The three Judys have just what you need to de-claw.

Southern Judy spills her southern sisters' secrets to soft and younger looking hands. Believe it or not, those southern girls use their buttermilk for more than biscuits. She also prescribes a good cream that diminishes those nasty spots we can no longer call freckles. Lastly, Southern suggests getting a fat transplant—in our hands—if we have the money and body fat to spare.

"What's that?" you ask. Just keep reading.

I'm Spikey Judy, and I will give you tips for waking up tired hands and dealing with brittle fingernails. I'm going to insist that you always protect your hands, especially when cleaning or gardening. Yes, I will bring up that E word again—exercise. However, hand exercises can be performed while watching TV or lying in bed. As with the feet, the hands contain a lot of nerve endings, so these exercises will feel really good. Finally, being from California—you know, all those fruits and nuts—I'll share some nutritional advice. I'm here to tell you that a diet rich in certain foods can do wonders for the hands, and especially the fingernails.

Sassy Judy addresses our tender hands and gives us tips for their ongoing nurture and care. Her tips are also easy on the wallet. Sunscreen is not just for the face, she explains. She also details how different kinds of moisturizers soothe our tender digits. She challenges us to begin using paraffin wax at home or at the salon, and then tells us why we should keep up our manicures. Sassy also shares how one professional hand model keeps her hands looking perfect.

Here's the sum of our advice: Put some time and effort into beautifying your hands. Make it a habit to protect, moisturize, exercise and eat healthy foods. Don't skip the manicures—you never know who might want to shake your hand. After all, you deserve to wear that five-carat diamond ring and show it off—why else would you want one?

JUDY

How to Treat Your Hands Like a Lady

By Southern Judy

"As you grow older, you will discover that you have two hands, one for helping yourself, and one for helping others."
—Audrey Hepburn, British actress and humanitarian

Years ago, I found that the sash on the back of one of my dresses was too difficult to tie by myself, and oh, how hard I tried. Then I felt someone's stronger and bigger hands reach down and tie the most beautiful and perfect bow at the back of my dress.

Not much has changed in that area of my strong will. It seems I still want to do it myself without any hands helping me. Through the years, I've learned that our hands are here to help—tie a sash, smooth a brow, ease a sorrow. We need to treat our hands as well as we've learned to treat each other.

When I think of my first memory of treated hands, my mind goes way back to helping my grandmother pick blackberries. Wanting to help, I would reach in and prick my finger and squeeze the berries. How her hands could grasp a berry without moving the leaves amazed me. Then I would look down and see hers and my grandfather's hands, darkened from working in the fields. She never complained about what the hard work had done to her soft skin, because she'd learned from her mother to treat her hands with a tiny bit of lard, rubbing it into her hands until it disappeared.

That tiny bit of hand treatment has come a long way. Nowadays, we are drawn into a specialty shop by the aromas that seem to reach out and pull us in as we walk by. There before our eyes are the most wonderful, silky hand creams—all calling, *Pick me, pick me!* Each one has a list of ingredients swearing to be the best of the best magic we can buy. All jars promise to treat our hands better than the last bottle we picked up.

Spend what you will, we Southerners know for a fact that we have the answer to the best treatment for hands. Aunt Nellie says her dainty hands, and I might add nearly ageless, are all due to a buttermilk soak and some of Pete's Stop-N-Go lotion. She rubs this in at night, and then sleeps in white cotton gloves. You know, she says her hands won first prize at the Tulip City State Fair. That blue ribbon still hangs proudly right over the pink bottles of Pete's lotion.

Although not a Southerner, Marilyn Monroe was said to have the most beautiful skin. As the story goes, Marilyn would bathe, rub Vaseline® all over and then sleep in thermal underwear. Many a night my husband, Mike, will ask about my white cotton socks. I'll put them on right after my bath, after I've rubbed some Vaseline all over my feet. Hey, if it was good enough for Marilyn Monroe...

Another option to get back younger-looking hands is more expensive, yet works great. Plastic surgeons can take fat from your body and insert it into the tops of your hands. Doctors say 50 percent will remain in your hands, therefore they tend to over-fill. That means your hands will be extra plump after surgery and then come down to a more normal size. Should you have need of a fat donor I have plenty to share, I'm just saying. There is also the option of laser treatments to remove brown spots and rejuvenate your hands. You can learn more about that in Sassy's chapter.

Some suggestions for treating your hands like a lady:

- **Wrap them up.** Cotton gloves and socks are a treat you should give yourself. Try some Vaseline just before bedtime, it will show you care about those hard working, busy hands and feet.
- **Try some leg-work on your hands.** Joan Rivers has a product called *Right to Bare Legs®*. It's a makeup for your legs that works perfectly on your hands. It is long-lasting and you will need to remove it with soap and water. This cover-up hides a multitude of age spots.

JUDY

Wake Up
Your Tired Hands

By Spikey Judy

*"Our hands play such an important role in our lives,
yet aside from manicures we really don't pay
that much attention to them."*
—Essie Weingarten, American founder and owner
of Essie® Nail Products

Recently, I attended the Fab Over Fifty Beauty Bash event in New York City. I was honored and thrilled to meet Essie, the founder of an amazing nail polish company. After posing for a picture with the three Judys, Essie asked if we were going to get the complimentary manicure her company was offering. I mumbled something incoherent under my breath, while discreetly hiding my hands. The last thing I wanted was for this goddess of nail care to see my tired hands.

My hands are so worn out that a palm reader has to double check to make sure she is not reading the lines *on top* of my hands. I have slow-growing, brittle nails and fast-growing, thick cuticles. The spots on my hands are too big to call freckles and over the last year, my knuckles have expanded so much I have trouble with ring sizes. I've also added new stress to my hands through my choice of extracurricular activities: boxing, horseback riding and hobbies that involve sewing and sharp needles.

Enough excuses. It's time to wake up these tired hands through prevention, exercise and nutrition.

Protect your hands while you work and play. If you are one of the unfortunate few like me who still clean their own home, wear rubber gloves. Despite what Madge of Palmolive® fame told you, household cleaners and dish soap are extremely damaging to the skin. If a product is designed to remove grease from the kitchen, it will definitely strip the moisture from your hands. Use gardening gloves for yard work and make sure to protect your hands when working out. I love to box, so I add pieces of foam under my hand wraps to protect the thin skin on my knuckles. This way I can still throw a hard punch without damaging the skin. If you like to pump iron, invest in a good pair of fingerless weight lifting gloves.

While you are pumping iron or doing other exercises, add in some routines specifically targeted for the hands and fingers. Working the muscles in the hands can keep them looking supple. Handgrips are good for strengthening the entire hand, but avoid too much resistance. The last thing we need are bigger knuckles. Instead opt for a squeeze ball. These feel good and have the added bonus of alleviating stress. Throughout the day, make an effort to stretch your fingers. Tighten your hand into a fist, then open up your fingers and stretch them out and up. After any workout, elevate your hands by propping on a pillow. Cold compresses will also help reduce any puffiness.

Lastly, feed your nails. Eat a diet rich in lean protein, zinc, iron, calcium and vitamins A, B and C. Nails are made of protein, so adding more protein to your diet will aid growth. A shortage of zinc causes those white marks on the nail surface, and a lack of iron results in those annoying ridges. Calcium will prevent brittle nails and vitamins A and B will keep nails from looking dull and dry. The lack of vitamin C encourages the growth of hangnails, so be sure to add citrus to your diet.

Stop picking on your cuticles and wake up your tired hands with prevention, exercise and diet. Your hands are the one part of your body that you see the most, so take the time to improve the view.

JUDY

Tender Hands: Like Tender Hearts, Treat Them Gently

By Sassy Judy

"Strength is the capacity to break a chocolate bar into four pieces with your bare hands—and then eat just one of the pieces."
—Judith Viorst, American author and columnist

We may be able to have youth in our facelifts, but our hands show our age. I'll say my hands are the maps of my life. My hands have played millions of keys on a piano, typed thousands of words at a computer and baked just one single blueberry pie. I have to thank my hands for giving me a career in New York City as a pianist and singer. I have a lot to thank my hands for doing—and not doing. Now when I look at my hands, I see tender hands in need of nurturing and care.

How does one care for hands that are tired and worn? Many of us will succumb to arthritis, carpal tunnel syndrome and tendinitis as we age. These conditions are treatable yet bothersome and can put a restraining order on any and all hand beauty treatments. As we age, the skin on our hands becomes thinner, less elastic and the veins grow more prominent. The goal is to treat our hands with helpers that are budget-friendly as much as possible before considering more invasive treatments. Here are some tips packed with promise.

- **Sunscreen.** The skin on the backs of our hands is much thinner than on our faces. Slathering on a good sunscreen a few times a day can definitely slow the signs of aging. Protect your hands from the sun as much as possible while outside. Use gloves to garden, bike, play tennis and golf. Sunscreens also help soften those ugly freckles known as brown spots or age spots. If age spots become a sore spot, you can try hydroquinone cream. You can buy this at any drugstore. Be sure to follow up with sunscreen to minimize discoloration. This two-step process takes patience and persistence but the rewards are in the hands!

- **Inexpensive creams.** Moisturizing your hands several times a day won't turn back the clock but, it certainly can improve the appearance of withered hands. Use products containing shea butter, olive oil, nut oils, glycerin or vitamin E oil. You can even use good old A&D ointment—the same thing used on babies' butts to treat diaper rash. These products protect and penetrate the skin, creating the illusion of plumper, more youthful hands. Apply creams immediately after washing, while your hands are still damp. This helps lock in those moisturizing benefits.

- **Wax wellness.** If you don't mind do-it-yourself kits, treat yourself to an at-home paraffin hand bath. Wax produces an extra coating that lasts longer and keeps hands smoother than creams. If you can't be bothered with at-home treatments, ask for it at your nail salon. An occasional paraffin pampering is a true pleasure.

- **Manicures.** When I first moved to New York, I met a gal who was a hand model. What she went through to keep her hands perfect was truly amazing. She kept her hands tipped at a ninety-degree angle from her elbows. This kept the blood flowing away from her hands, thus reducing the appearance of veins. She wore white cotton gloves during the summer and winter, adding warm gloves over the cotton ones when the days grew cold. She claimed the white cotton kept her skin color more uniform. Plus, she always had a manicure. As a hand model, part of her job was having manicures every day to advertise a new product. Even so, not one time did she go to an audition without a proper manicure. I guess one could say her income was truly a hand out!

Here's a handsome idea, ladies. Keep your hands to yourself only if you like what you see. Otherwise, try inexpensive alternatives before more expensive treatments such as fillers, laser treatments and so on. Nothing makes the hands look more groomed than a manicure. I love the gel manicures because they last up to two weeks. These are worth the price because chipping is *finito*.

One more tip, ladies—your nails are jewels, not tools. Don't use your nails to pry lids off jars or scrape crud off the carpet. Respect your hands and nails—and they will help you defy your age.

Southern Says...

JUDY

- Southern girls know that Vaseline® and white gloves go to bed together.
- Don't forget to use makeup to cover a spot or two on your hands. People notice your hands more than you think.
- Hands tell age, keep yours manicured and hydrated with lotion.
- A nifty new miracle hand cream is available from a former hand model. It's called Ellen Sirot's Hand Perfection®.

Spikey Says...

JUDY

- Like the look of gloves, and live in a warmer climate? Try fingerless gloves.
- For artistic nail designs without the high cost and fuss, try Sally Hansen® Salon Effects. These are actually strips of nail polish that you can put directly onto your nails. They come in a variety of colors and fun designs. Plus, they are easy to apply and long-lasting.
- If your knuckles have enlarged and you can't get your rings off, visit a good jeweler and ask for a ring expander.

Sassy Says...

JUDY

- Fillers aren't just for faces anymore. Ask about the latest for hands.
- Butt fat transferred into your hands (like feet) to plump up those bulging veins? Believe it.
- Never underestimate the properties of olive oil. It's cheap and effective.
- Got rings to show off? Get manicure first.

Inner Work, Outer Work or the Heck with Work?

"I exercise, run my mouth, push my luck
and jump to conclusions!"
—Author Unknown

Every day we ponder what we would like our body to look like, think like and act like. Then we get our second cup of coffee and look in the mirror. We drop our bathrobe and after the initial shock hits, we promise ourselves, this is the day I will make a difference in how my body looks!

It is not that we intend to give up and allow our fat cells to win—that's what happens when we do nothing to stop it.

In this chapter, Spikey says our inner goddess speaks for us in how we act and dream. She has us pegged in her thoughts about our inner goddess. Way to go Spikey!

Sassy says play dates are fun and mentions her pretty mom staying in shape at her young age of 90! Sassy says dancing is another way to stay in shape, to that I say Amen!

My advice to you is this: It is time to get up off the couch and make it work no matter the pain, sweat and tears. Who said it was easy? Probably that Sarah Marie! According to her, whom I might add has the body of a teen and a butt you could crack an egg on, "All a body has to do is get up and do a few exercises and run 15 miles a day." Although I hate to admit it, she is right. Just look at her, it's almost enough to make me give up chocolate. What was I thinking? There is nothing on God's earth better than chocolate. Maybe tomorrow I can try eating one or two fewer cookies and skip my cup of ice cream on Sunday.

Walking is a start to better health and thinner thighs, so they say. We could also start with an inner search of our true self. That's what Patty Jo says during her Yoga of Peace workshops held at the Tulip Curl Up If You Can Center in my home town. Why, you can hear moans and groans that would make Aunt Nellie blush coming out of that place. Just walk by when Patty Jo opens the windows precisely at 10:00 a.m. and you'll see almost every man in the county, as they just happen to be coming that way. Honestly, some of those poses are worse than childbirth. You cannot wear just anything to the class. No, it has to be pink and skintight because Patty Jo says we have to be able to see our body working. My advice, don't get downwind of Mary Beth, if you know what I mean. Now I know why Patty Jo keeps the windows open.

Truth is that there is a thinner, trimmer body inside us just wanting to come out. We do not have to settle for the middle age bulge. There comes a time when you have to fight for the body you want, not give in and accept the way it looks today. Sure it is a walk, maybe a jog, or a full-blown run that will be our way out of the body we are in right now. Trouble is after supper and getting the dishes all washed and put away, the couch and TV look so tempting. I promise, tomorrow I will start my exercise program. Now if I can only remember where I put my sneakers.

JUDY

Exercise, Sexercise and Mesmerize!

By Southern Judy

"Ability is what you are capable of doing. Motivation determines what you do. Attitude determines how well you do it."
—Lou Holtz, American retired football coach, sportscaster and motivational speaker

It has been said that half the battle is won just by making up your mind and getting off the couch. That's good advice. Right now I am looking at a funny sign I have in my studio that reads, "Exercise? I thought you said accessorize." Many of us boomers share this feeling when it comes to moving our bodies. We have the best of intentions, but when the weather gets colder, or it starts to rain, or we are just too tired today, the message we hear is *maybe tomorrow*. Truth is it is difficult to exercise and making time for it is something we just don't put on our calendar, at least not regularly.

Two is a couple and three is a crowd simply does not apply to exercise. More people around to get us up and moving is the best incentive on earth. But for girls in the South, something cute to work out in would probably be enough for us to get out and about and in full makeup no doubt! Why waste a completely cute outfit by staying inside?

Just last week, while a few of the girls were having a cold glass of peach tea on my porch, the topic came up about some of us putting on a few pounds. No one dared look around, but each of us thought we were talking about Mary Lou. Certainly not about me, why I can still wear my cheerleading outfit! Recently, in a fun night, well, maybe I shouldn't say any more. . .It still fits, I'm just saying.

Anyway, Mary Lou led the march to Pete's Stop-N-Go in search of something to wear while exercising. One by one we slipped inside to look at what Pete had to offer. Well, girl we put out an alert that was heard all over town. Soon Pete's Stop-N-Go was calling everywhere to supply us with that cute set. Honestly, I swore never to repeat who needed that XXL size.

It did not take long to get our husbands involved, just a quick look at our cute workout suits and they were more than willing to help us get out the door. May I say that my husband, Mike, is watching his weight? He is afraid he and John Henry will be next in line for the *Lose a Gut* book we saw on TV last night. There is nothing wrong with involving our mates in an exercise program—it can be fun for both—so long as we can make it an inside sport as well.

At age forty, we start the battle of the bulge, then at fifty we gather our weapons, and at sixty we declare an all-out war against fat and cellulite. Tell me—does pole dancing count as exercise? Just asking...

Exercise is important for your health, your figure *and* your closet!
- How would you like to look younger? It all starts with losing those extra pounds that keep us out of the smaller sized clothing we so love to wear.

- Help your closet lose weight by getting rid of those clothes you wore five years ago. Clothing that fits too tight makes us look like we weigh more than we do. Plus, it's all out of style—what's the point of losing weight if you're going around town in old clothes?

JUDY

Your Inner Goddess is Jumping for Joy!

By Spikey Judy

"Through the Goddess, we can discover our strength, enlighten our minds, own our bodies, and celebrate our emotions."
—Starhawk, American writer and activist

We have heard that real beauty comes from the inside out. All women are unique and sacred beings—goddesses. In traditional lore, the goddess manifests in three ways: the maiden, the mother and the crone. Each one represents the different phases of womanhood.

Excuse me? We are baby boomers. Most of us left our maidenhood in Woodstock, we either had no children or the children are grown up, and if anyone calls us a crone, we'll smack them. Therefore, dear reader, I am inviting you to redefine your sacred self. To help you on your way, I will be exploring the manifestations of the three Judys—Southern, Spikey and Sassy.

Southern

You are the epitome of a lady. Gracious, warm and welcoming. You attract people to you and total strangers will strike up a conversation as if they have known you all of their lives. You are a romantic and will always leave your partner with a smile on his face. Your favorite movie is *Somewhere in Time* because, for you, love transcends time and space. Your idea of a perfect evening out is a romantic dinner for two followed by a horse and buggy ride. However, you are not all soft, mushy and frilly. You can be very protective of those you love and are definitely capable of "bringing home the bacon and frying it up in the pan." The Southern goddess's style icons are Princess Diana, Doris Day and Grace Kelly. Their looks are timeless and classic. If money were no object, you would hire Carolina Herrera to design your personal wardrobe. Her classy and feminine looks are made for you.

Spikey

You are edgy, intense and in possession of an extreme and twisted sense of humor. You are an artist at heart, one who relates more to Salvador Dali than Monet. Your idea of a romantic evening out is riding your Harley®, watching a good boxing match and slam dancing the night away. Your favorite movies are *A Clockwork Orange* and *Monty Python and the Holy Grail* because for you, nothing is sacred. You love animals, yet are terrified of small children. Spikey style icons are Bianca Jagger, Cher and Lady Gaga. You crave a closet full of Alexander McQueen® and Christian Seriano® fashions, yet are more apt to hunt down that yet unknown and totally unique designer.

Sassy

You are the ultimate New York City girl who can easily flag down a taxi while wearing stilettos. You've got legs and the attitude to match. You like to be in charge and when not being called *sassy*, prefer to be addressed as *the Queen*. However, you are very approachable and like to know people as well as being known. You are comfortable in front of a camera and always photogenic. Your idea of a perfect evening out is a Broadway show and dinner at Sardis. Your favorite movie is *Gentlemen Prefer Blondes* because it's funny and who doesn't prefer blondes! Sassy fashion icons are Catherine Zeta-Jones, Audrey Hepburn and Marlene Dietrich. Their dramatic, yet poised, appearances mirror your own. You have the haute couture vibe and deserve to be dressed in the latest Yves Saint Laurent®, Valentino® and Marc Jacobs®.

We all have our own unique inner goddess. Yours might be a little Southern, Spikey or Sassy or maybe more Spicy, Sultry or Sporty. Whoever you are, let your inner self sing and dance. Celebrating ourselves is the ultimate beauty treatment!

JUDY

Play Dates, Play Mates— Never Placate!

By Sassy Judy

"To find joy in work is to discover the fountain of youth."
—Pearl S. Buck, American author and Pulitzer Prize winner

My mother never talks of retiring—instead she tells everyone she is recycling! She learned from me to *never give up your day job*. At the age of 89, she retired as a floor nurse at a major hospital in Virginia to work with an organ donor foundation. Never one to sit idle, she volunteers her time, visits friends, travels and still drives. She takes no medications. I'm proud to resemble my mother. We have the same eyes, boobs and legs. With her newfound "retirement" she has taken up walking. The result? She has lost so much weight she has room for twins in her favorite, bury-me-in-this, blue dress. Talk about playing, my mother has a play mate called life!

All of us would love to be in our eighties with such a healthy lifestyle. Some of us would like to have a more active lifestyle in our forties. However, the reality is as we age, we start to slow down, sit down and settle down. We get comfortable with life as usual and won't try anything new.

Ladies, giving in to middle age woes is worse than getting trapped in a high-rise elevator. Just don't go there. When was the last time you made a date with a friend you haven't seen in a good while? We flirt with the idea, but do we really get around to doing it? When was the last time you danced with your mate? Is that even a thought? When did you last change your exercise routine? I see loads of people at the gym doing the old familiar workout, frustrated with the same results. Same body mass, different day. The older we get, the more we resist change. That means you have to challenge yourself. It's a fact that as we age we have to work harder to stay fit in mind, body and soul. How can we shake up the monotony?

- **Dare yourself.** Step outside of your comfort zone and do something wild. I took up dirty dancing in the form of pole dancing and I love it. Try something you have always wanted to do and felt you couldn't. Give yourself permission to visit your silly side. Don't judge yourself. Find your fun side.
- **Retire *to* something.** Have a plan for the next step in life. The people who age the fastest are the ones who retire and go from

doing something to doing nothing. There are plenty of innovation and reinvention courses that will enlighten and motivate you. Check out the annual Reinvention Convention sponsored by *More*® magazine.

- **Laugh, love and live.** We take ourselves too seriously. Maturity does not mean moldy. Lighten up when it comes to political issues, family issues, money issues and health issues. Having a strong will and good attitude can get you through life's cancers. Love the ones you can and release those who won't accept your love. Life is an orchestra and you are the conductor. Play with passion.

Above all, be the cheerleader for your own game of life. Don't sit on the sidelines. Midlife deals us a new deck of cards. Romance the Jacks, marry the Kings, always be the Queen and have a big, beautiful heart. After all, *getting older never looked so good!*

Southern Says... JUDY

- Puzzles, games, anything with a challenge, broadens our minds.
- Ignore the weather, go for a walk. It is great for your body.
- "Never give up, Never give up, Never give up," Winston Churchill's great advice that he gave to a graduating class, still good today!
- Embrace your inner artist. Take a drawing, painting, ceramics, jewelry or other creative class.

Spikey Says... JUDY

- Facing retirement and don't know what to do with yourself? Consider volunteering. It is very fulfilling and very social.
- Make exercise fun. I ride horses which can burn close to 300 calories per hour!
- Don't think of a diet as losing weight. Most of us want to find something we've lost. Instead, think of it as donating fat to starving models.
- Say yes to sex. Plan play dates with your partner. No partner? Set aside an evening just for you. Candlelight, bubble bath and extra batteries.

Sassy Says... JUDY

- We work out our body why not our brain? Sleep on the opposite side of your bed, color with your opposite hand, button your coat with opposite fingers. Read *Super Brains* by Deepak Chopra and Rudolf E. Tanzi, 2012. It's like closet clearing for the brain.
- Laugh until tears stream down your face.
- Love what you do or don't do it!
- Find your soul's goal. Your inner voice is singing. Listen to the melody and harmonize with it! Sweet sounds.

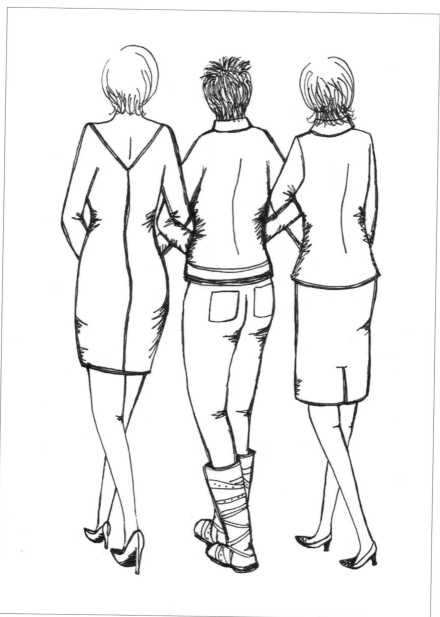

The 3 Judys—friends to the end!

Judith Taylor, AICI, CIP
615-773-5341
looknyrbst@aol.com
judith@stylemanagement4u.com
www.stylemanagement4u.com

Judith is the sparkle that makes the stars shine in Nashville! Helping them put their best boot forward, she brings glamour and style to entertainers as well as individuals and corporate clients. Her clients come in once and stay with her for a lifetime.

Since 1995, Judith has been an internationally recognized expert in her industry. She was the fashion editor for the Nashville Newsletter and writes for newspapers and magazines, including the Association of Image Consultants International. She hosts a radio show, Looking Your Best Off Music Row, on the prestigious Music Row in Nashville. Judith is frequently in and out of radio and TV studios. She is a regular on the Bridges show, and she is also a dynamic and entertaining sought after speaker, adding her down-to-earth, distinctive flavor of energy and fun while lighting up the room and captivating audiences.

Judith developed her own skin care and cosmetic line in 1996, making it easy for her clients to look their best. Along with her previous books, *My Style, My Way* and *Freeing Godiva,* she infuses her latest book with her southern charm, wit and humor while sharing tips and insights on getting older and looking good!

Judith Ann Graham, CIP
1-800-NYC-LOOK (692-5665)
jag@judithanngraham.com
www.judithanngraham.com

JUDY

Judith Ann Graham, a former Miss New York State in the Miss America Organization, is a personal wardrobe stylist and makeup expert. A native Virginian, Judith began her career in New York as a singer/pianist performing at landmark hotels. This soon earned her the nick name, *Judith, Queen of the Lobbies*. While performing at night, she spent her days polishing her talent as an actress, landing several roles in television commercials and daytime dramas including *All My Children*.

Having learned from the best stylists and makeup artists in the business, Judith naturally reinvented herself as a style expert. She has been featured on CBS, FOX, NBC, ABC and *Late Night with David Letterman*. Judith's passion for makeup, particularly airbrush makeup artistry, has earned her the title, *Beauty by Judy* of the bridal business. She is co-author of *Image Power* and author of *My Bride Guide—a Wedding Planner for Your Personal Style*.

Judith is a certified professional image consultant and is an award recipient having served on both local an international image consulting boards. She is also a member of Fashion Group International and teaches wedding planning and makeup artistry at the Fashion Institute of Technology.

Judith Herbert

Verve Image Consulting
…because there is an "I" in Image
805-624-7620
judy@judyherbert.com
www.judyherbert.com

Judith Herbert is a life-long fashionista and founder of Verve Image Consulting. She specializes in helping people discover and showcase their complete selves by teaching them how to put the "I" into *image*. She offers a "whole-istic" approach to image by addressing the inner self and how it relates to the individual's outer appearance. Her clients look better, feel healthier and gain increased awareness and self-confidence to live extraordinary lives.

Judith brings a wide range of professional and personal experience to enhance her clients' needs. Having earned a bachelor of science in construction management, she provides a sound foundation of planning, time management and business finance to better serve her clients. Judith moved on to acquire a master's degree (awarded magna cum laude) focusing on women's roles in society.

She belongs to Vista Point Artists—a Southern California artist collective. This unique combination of business and creative skills profoundly impacts her image business and the clients she serves. In addition, Judith is designated as a certified life and wellness coach. A native Californian, Judith's motto is, "Sound strategies create expressive new lives."

Getting Older Never Looked So Good

Get Your Glam On!
(Ask the three Judys how it's done.)

When you look in the mirror, do you see dumpy or diva? Do you know the secrets to looking ten years younger? Would you like to dress ten pounds slimmer? Do you say yes to the dress only to hear no from your gal pals?

If you need answers to the questions you didn't know to ask, then you're just a finger-click away from get-you-gorgeous advice.

Sign up for your FREE online Style File at www.3judys.com.
Our Style File is packed with monthly tips on how to look and feel like the superstar you are! Send us a photo of yourself and we will give you a style analysis. You'll also be entered to win a tube of our exclusive Beautiful Babe (BB) Lipstick.

Southern Judy, Spikey Judy and Sassy Judy are the nifty-over-fifty ladies who bring the class and sass to everyday decisions on what to wear and how to wear it. We'll even challenge you to ask: *why not wear it?*

We are the three Judys, and while we share the same name, that's where the similarities end. Southern Judy oozes charm and elegance with her classic take on style and fashion. Spikey Judy intoxicates us with an edgy, artistic flair. Sassy Judy lures us to center stage with show stopping glamour.

Whatever style you favor—even if it's time to update your look—you are sure to relate to the three Judys.

The 3 Judys are experts on such topics as:
- Makeup and hair
- Closet shopping
- Lifestyle transitions
- Universal style types
- Shape analysis
- Color assessment
- Cyber styling (Send us a photo and we'll style you.)
- Skype styling (Book a Skype session for a style assessment.)
- Wardrobe selection and management
- Accessory enhancement
- Special occasion dressing
- Casual confident dressing

If you'd like to look your best at any age, sign up for your FREE online Style File at www.3judys.com.

Southern Judy, Spikey Judy and Sassy Judy are available to speak at your corporate event, leadership event, business group, women's focus group or club, television, radio and internet opportunities.

Contact
www.3judys.com
Facebook: facebook.com/3judys
Twitter: twitter.com/3judys

Email
southern@3judys.com
spikey@3judys.com
sassy@3judys.com

Phone
1-800-NYC-LOOK (692-5665)

3JUDYS
SOUTHERN \ \ SPIKEY \ \ SASSY

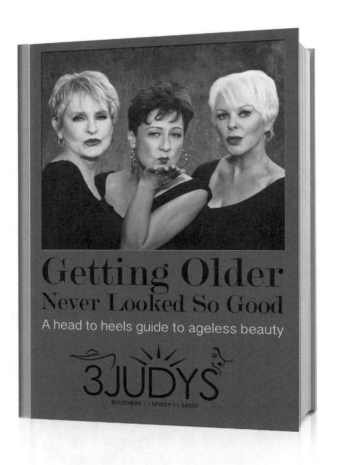

For more copies of this book,

Getting Older Never Looked So Good...
A head to heels guide to ageless beauty

contact Southern, Spikey or Sassy at
www.3judys.com
southern@, spikey@, sassy@3judys.com
1-800-NYC-LOOK
USA